# 101 Quick & Easy Cross-Stitch Projects

the Needlecraft Shop

Product Development Director   CAROLYN CHRISTMAS
Publishing Services Manager   ANGE VAN ARMAN
Editor   NANCY HARRIS
Product Development Staff   TONYA FLYNN
DARLA HASSELL
ALICE MITCHELL
Assistant Editor   SHIRLEY BROWN
MICHELLE HUDSON
MARYLEE KLINKHAMMER
Copy Editor   SHIRLEY PATRICK
Book Design   GREG SMITH
Production Artist   JOANNE GONZALEZ
Photography Supervisor   SCOTT CAMPBELL
Photographer   ANDY J. BURNFIELD
Photo Stylist   MARTHA COQUAT
Photo Assistant   CRYSTAL KEY
Production Coordinator   GLENDA CHAMBERLAIN

Chief Executive Officer   JOHN ROBINSON
Marketing Director   SCOTT MOSS

Customer Service   1-800-449-0440
Pattern Services   (903) 636-5140

### CREDITS
Sincerest thanks to all the designers,
manufacturers and other professionals
whose dedication has made this book possible.

### Special thanks to
Quebecor Printing Book Group, Kingsport, Tennessee

Library of Congress Cataloging-in-Publication Data
ISBN: 1-57367-119-3
First Printing: 2001
Library of Congress Catalog Card Number:
2001119042
Published and Distributed by
The Needlecraft Shop, Big Sandy, Texas 75755
Printed in the United States of America.

Visit us at **NeedlecraftShop.com**

Do you ever feel like your day-to-day schedule is packed from morning till night? Do you wish you had more time to pursue your true love — cross-stitch? Then this collection of designs is just for you. This book is filled with fast-and-fun favorites, each and every one chosen to fit cross-stitch into your busy days. You'll find plenty of ideas on the following pages, such as projects for every room of your home, exceptional fashions for the young and old, designs for holidays throughout the year and unique projects for memorable days. Each of these all-new designs will be a delight to make and share with family and friends.

Gather up your fabric and floss and get ready for stitching fun. This collection of designs was chosen for stitchers of every skill level, and each can be completed with a minimum of time. Best of all, although they don't take long to make, these projects look so great you'll proudly say you made them yourself.

*Nancy*

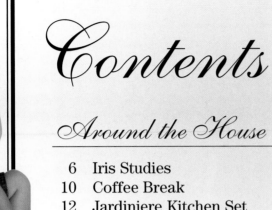

# Contents

## Around the House

## Fabulous Fashions

## Happy Holidays

## Special Days

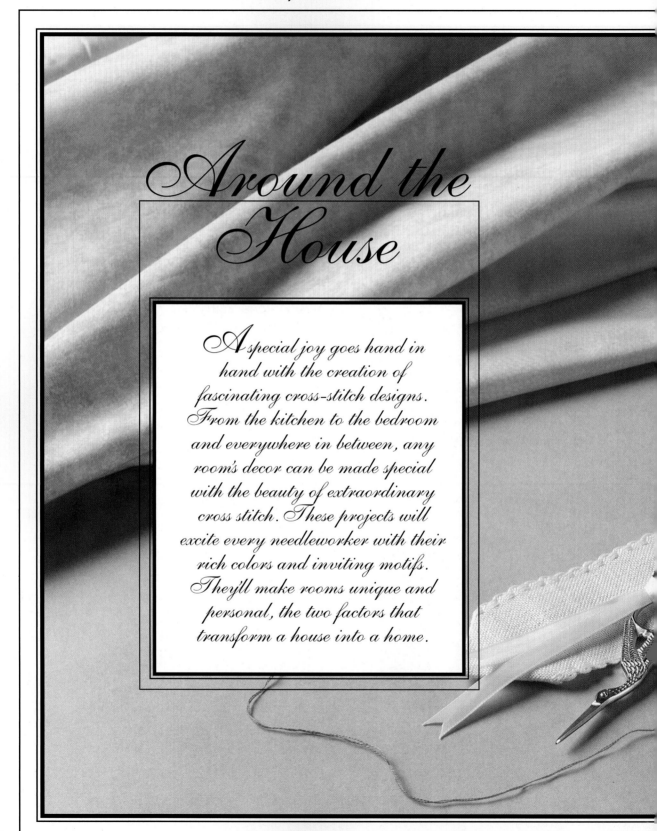

# Chapter One

# Around the House

A special joy goes hand in hand with the creation of fascinating cross-stitch designs. From the kitchen to the bedroom and everywhere in between, any room's decor can be made special with the beauty of extraordinary cross stitch. These projects will excite every needleworker with their rich colors and inviting motifs. They'll make rooms unique and personal, the two factors that transform a house into a home.

# Iris Studies

## DESIGNED BY JULIA LUCAS

*Start them today, finish them tonight! These pretty needlework accessories are what every stitcher needs.*

## Materials

- One 5¾" x 8" piece (for Pincushion) and one 10" x 10" piece (for Needlesafe) of cream 36-count Edinburgh linen
- 54" piece of cream 2"-wide 30-count Linen Stitchband (for Chatelaine)
- Wooden pincushion with 3¾"-round design area
- Felt
- ½ yd. ribbon
- Two ⅞" rings

## Instructions

1: For Pincushion, center and stitch "Blue Iris Bunch" design onto 5¾" x 8" piece of Edinburgh, stitching over two threads and using two strands floss for Cross-Stitch and one strand floss for Backstitch. Assemble pincushion following man-ufacturer's instructions.

2: For Needlesafe, beginning 1¼" from right short edge, center and stitch "Mauve Iris Bunch" design onto 10" x 10" piece of Edinburgh, stitching over two threads and using two strands floss for Cross-Stitch and one strand floss for Backstitch.

Notes: From felt, cut one 10" x 10" piece for backing. From ribbon, cut two 6" pieces for ties. Use ¼" seam allowance.

3: With right sides facing, baste one end of each tie to center of short edges of design. With right sides facing, sew design and backing together, leaving a small opening. Turn right sides out; slip stitch opening closed.

4: For Chatelaine, center and stitch two "Mauve Iris Single" and one "Blue Iris Single" designs onto one end of Stitchband positioning as desired, stitching over two threads and using two strands floss for Cross-Stitch and one strand floss for Backstitch. Center and

stitch "Mauve Iris Duo" and "Blue Iris Duo" designs onto other end of Stitchband positioning as desired, stitching over two threads and using two strands floss for Cross-Stitch and one strand floss for Backstitch.

Note: Cut remaining ribbon in half.

5: Tack rings to each end of chatelaine as shown in photo. Secure ribbons to rings as shown.

**Blue Iris Bunch and Mauve Iris Bunch Stitch Count:**
34 wide x 32 high

**Approximate Design Size:**
11-count 3⅛" x 3"
14-count 2½" x 2⅜"
16-count 2⅛" x 2"
18-count 2" x 1⅞"
22-count 1⅝" x 1½"
36-count over two threads 2" x 1⅞"

**Blue Iris Single and Mauve Iris Single Stitch Count:**
22 wide x 19 high

**Approximate Design Size:**
11-count 2" x 1¾"
14-count 1⅝" x 1⅜"
16-count 1⅜" x 1¼"
18-count 1¼" x 1⅛"
22-count 1" x ⅞"
30-count over two threads 1½" x 1⅜"

**Blue Iris Duo and Mauve Iris Duo Stitch Count:**
32 wide x 23 high

**Approximate Design Size:**
11-count 3" x 2⅛"
14-count 2⅜" x 1¾"
16-count 2" x 1½"
18-count 1⅞" x 1⅜"
22-count 1½" x 1⅛"
30-count over two threads 1⅞" x 1⅝"

### Mauve Iris Single

### Mauve Iris Bunch

### Mauve Iris Duo

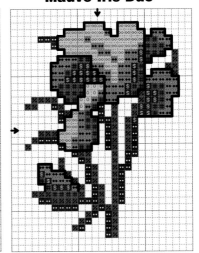

### Mauve Iris

| X | B'st | DMC® | ANCHOR® | COLORS |
|---|------|------|---------|--------|
| # | | 208 | 110 | Very Dk. Lavender |
| •• | | 209 | 109 | Dk. Lavender |
| ∞ | | 211 | 342 | Lt. Lavender |
| •• | | 319 | 218 | Very Dk. Pistachio Green |
| ∕ | | 367 | 217 | Dk. Pistachio Green |
| $ | — | 550 | 102 | Very Dk. Violet |
| ◊ | | 3822 | 295 | Lt. Straw |

### Blue Iris

| X | B'st | DMC® | ANCHOR® | COLORS |
|---|------|------|---------|--------|
| •• | | 319 | 218 | Very Dk. Pistachio Green |
| •• | | 340 | 118 | Med. Blue Violet |
| ∕ | | 367 | 217 | Dk. Pistachio Green |
| $ | — | 791 | 178 | Very Dk. Cornflower Blue |
| # | | 3746 | 1030 | Dk. Blue Violet |
| ∞ | | 3747 | 120 | Very Lt. Blue Violet |
| ◊ | | 3822 | 295 | Lt. Straw |

### Blue Iris Bunch

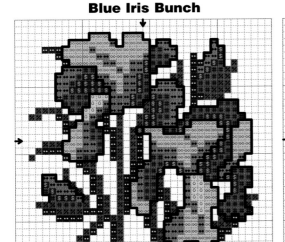

### Blue Iris Duo

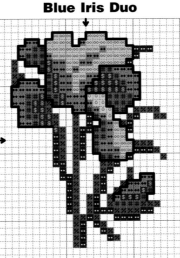

### Blue Iris Single

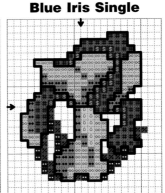

# Coffee Break

## DESIGNED BY JULIA LUCAS

*Glorious sunflowers burst into bloom on these lovely trivets. These bright and sunny coffee mug designs are sure to delight all coffee lovers.*

## Materials for One

- 11" x 11" piece of seafoam green 22-count Vienna
- Acrylic trivet with 5"-square design opening

## Instructions

1: Center and stitch design of choice, stitching over two threads and using four strands floss for Cross-Stitch and two strands floss for Backstitch.

2: Position and secure design in trivet following manufacturer's instructions.

**Mug 1**

**Mug 2**

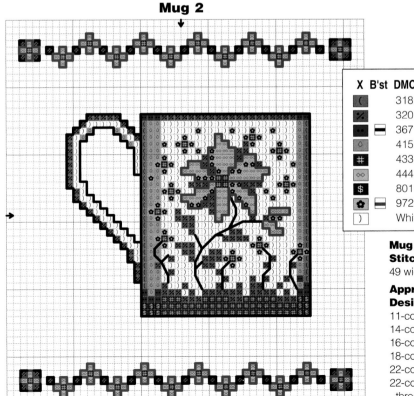

| X | B'st | DMC® | ANCHOR® | COLORS |
|---|------|------|---------|--------|
| ( | | 318 | 399 | Lt. Steel Gray |
| ⁒ | | 320 | 215 | Med. Pistachio Green |
| ▪ | ▬ | 367 | 217 | Dk. Pistachio Green |
| ◊ | | 415 | 398 | Pearl Gray |
| # | | 433 | 358 | Med. Brown |
| ∞ | | 444 | 290 | Dk. Lemon |
| $ | | 801 | 359 | Dk. Coffee Brown |
| ✿ | ▬ | 972 | 298 | Deep Canary |
| ) | | White | 2 | White |

**Mug 1 and Mug 2**
**Stitch Count:**
49 wide x 54 high

**Approximate Design Size:**
11-count 4½" x 5"
14-count 3½" x 3⅞"
16-count 3⅛" x 3⅜"
18-count 2¾" x 3"
22-count 2¼" x 2½"
22-count over two
  threads 4½" x 5"

# *Jardiniere Kitchen Set*

## DESIGNED BY HOPE MURPHY

**M**ake a matching place mat, napkin ring, pot holder, towel and valance with simple Country French motifs.

## *Materials*

• One 13½" x 20" piece (for Place Mat), one 14" x 52" piece (for Valance) and four 3" x 7" pieces (for Napkin Rings) of navy/cream 20-count Diana
• Hang towel with 3" white 14-count Aida insert
• Pot holder with 5½" x 7" white 14-count Aida insert
• 3⅛ yds. piping
• Lining fabric
• Eight ³⁄₁₆" snaps

## *Instructions*

1: For Place Mat front, center and stitch designs of choice onto 13½" x 20" piece of Diana following Place Mat Stitching Diagram, stitching over two threads and using two strands floss for Cross-Stitch.

Notes: From lining fabric, cut one 13½" x 20" piece. Use ½" seam allowance.

2: With right sides facing and piping between, sew Place Mat front and lining together, leaving an opening for turning. Turn right sides out; slip stitch opening closed; press.

3: For Valance, center and stitch designs of choice onto 14" x 52" piece of Diana following Valance Stitching Diagram, stitching over two threads and using two strands floss for Cross-Stitch.

4: Fold top edge down 1½" to wrong side; sew in place for rod pocket.

5: Fold bottom edge up 2" to wrong side; sew in place. Finish side edges.

6: For Napkin Rings, center and stitch each "Napkin Ring" design, onto each 3" x 7" piece of Diana, stitching over two threads and using two strands floss for Cross-Stitch.

Note: From lining fabric, cut four 3" x 7" pieces.

7: For each Napkin Ring, position and sew two snaps 1" from each short edge. With right sides facing, sew piping to long edges of each Napkin Ring. With right sides facing, sew Napkin Ring and lining together, leaving an opening for turning. Turn right sides out; slip stitch opening closed; press.

8: For Hang Towel, center and stitch "Towel" design, using two strands floss for Cross-Stitch.

9: For Pot Holder, center and stitch "Pot Holder" design, using two strands floss for Cross-Stitch.

## Valance Stitching Diagram

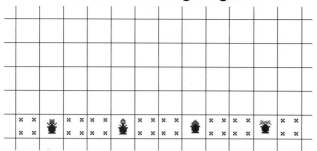

## Place Mat Stitching Diagram

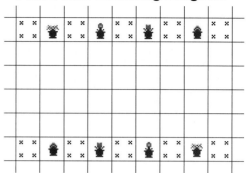

**Pink**
**Stitch Count:**
8 wide x 11 high

**Approximate**
**Design Size:**
11-count ¾" x 1"
14-count ⅝" x ⅞"
16-count ½" x ¾"
18-count ½" x ⅝"
22-count ⅜" x ½"
20-count over two
  threads ⅞" x 1⅛"

**Red**
**Stitch Count:**
10 wide x 11 high

**Approximate**
**Design Size:**
11-count 1" x 1"
14-count ¾" x ⅞"
16-count ⅝" x ¾"
18-count ⅝" x ⅝"
22-count ½" x ½"
20-count over two
  threads 1" x 1⅛"

**Orange**
**Stitch Count:**
8 wide x 12 high

**Approximate**
**Design Size:**
11-count ¾" x 1⅛"
14-count ⅝" x ⅞"
16-count ½" x ¾"
18-count ½" x ¾"
22-count ⅜" x ⅝"
20-count over two
  threads ⅞" x 1¼"

**Purple**
**Stitch Count:**
8 wide x 13 high

**Approximate**
**Design Size:**
11-count ¾" x 1¼"
14-count ⅝" x 1"
16-count ½" x ⅞"
18-count ½" x ¾"
22-count ⅜" x ⅝"
20-count over two
  threads ⅞" x 1¾"

**Towel**
**Stitch Count:**
172 wide x 38 high

**Approximate**
**Design Size:**
11-count 15⅝" x 3½"
14-count 12¼" x 2¾"
16-count 10¾" x 2⅜"
18-count 9⅝" x 2⅛"
22-count 7⅞" x 1¾"

| X | DMC® | ANCHOR® | COLORS |
|---|------|---------|--------|
| ↔ | 355 | 1014 | Dk. Terra Cotta |
| ▲ | 469 | 267 | Avocado Green |
| ◊ | 553 | 98 | Violet |
| ⁒ | 604 | 55 | Lt. Cranberry |
| $ | 608 | 332 | Bright Orange |
| # | 666 | 46 | Bright Red |
| ★ | 820 | 134 | Very Dk. Royal Blue |
| ( | 973 | 297 | Bright Canary |

**Block Pattern,**
**Red Napkin Ring,**
**Orange Napkin**
**Ring, Pink Napkin**
**Ring and Purple**
**Napkin Ring**
**Stitch Count:**
19 wide x 19 high

**Approximate**
**Design Size:**
11-count 1¾" x 1¾"
14-count 1⅜" x 1⅜"
16-count 1¼" x 1¼"
18-count 1⅛" x 1⅛"
22-count ⅞" x ⅞"
20-count over two
  threads 2" x 2"

## Pink Napkin Ring

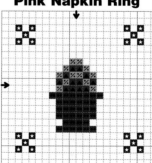

## Red Napkin Ring

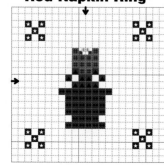

## Purple Napkin Ring

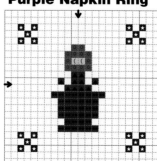

## Orange Napkin Ring

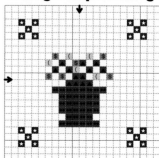

**Towel**

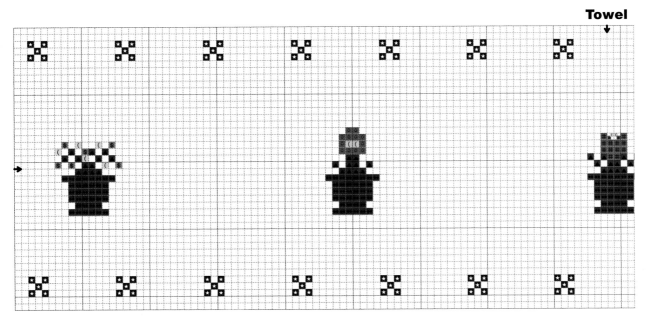

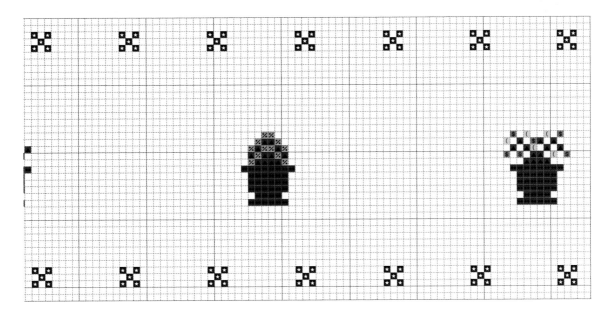

**Block Pattern**

**Pink**   **Red**   **Orange**   **Purple**

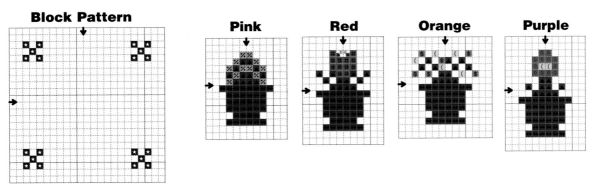

| X | DMC® | ANCHOR® | COLORS |
|---|------|---------|--------|
| ■ | 355 | 1014 | Dk. Terra Cotta |
| ▲ | 469 | 267 | Avocado Green |
| ρ | 553 | 98 | Violet |
| % | 604 | 55 | Lt. Cranberry |
| $ | 308 | 332 | Bright Orange |
| # | 666 | 46 | Bright Red |
| ★ | 820 | 134 | Very Dk. Royal Blue |
| ( | 973 | 297 | Bright Canary |

**Potholder
Stitch Count:**
94 wide x 76 high

**Approximate
Design Size:**
11-count 8⅝" x 7"
14-count 6¾" x 5½"
16-count 5⅞" x 4¾"
18-count 5¼" x 4¼"
22-count 4⅜" x 3½"

**Potholder**

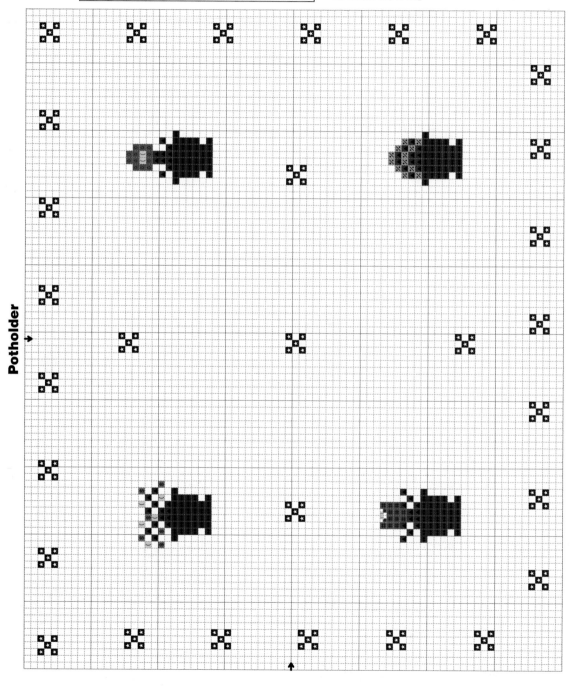

*101 Quick & Easy Cross-Stitch Projects*

# Safari Pillows

## DESIGNED BY ROSEMARY PADDEN

*Capture the majestic beauty of the African wildlife in spectacular stitchery! These dramatic designs work up quickly with extra-large stitches.*

## Materials for One

- One 19" x 19" piece of cream (for "Giraffe") or one 19" x 19" piece of white (for "Zebra") 14-count Lincoln
- ½ yd. fabric
- 1 yd. piping
- Fiberfill

## Instructions

1: Center and stitch design of choice, stitching over two threads and using six strands floss for Cross-Stitch.

**Giraffe**

| X | DMC® | ANCHOR® | COLORS |
|---|------|---------|--------|
| L | 3829 | 374 | Very Dk. Old Gold |

**Giraffe**

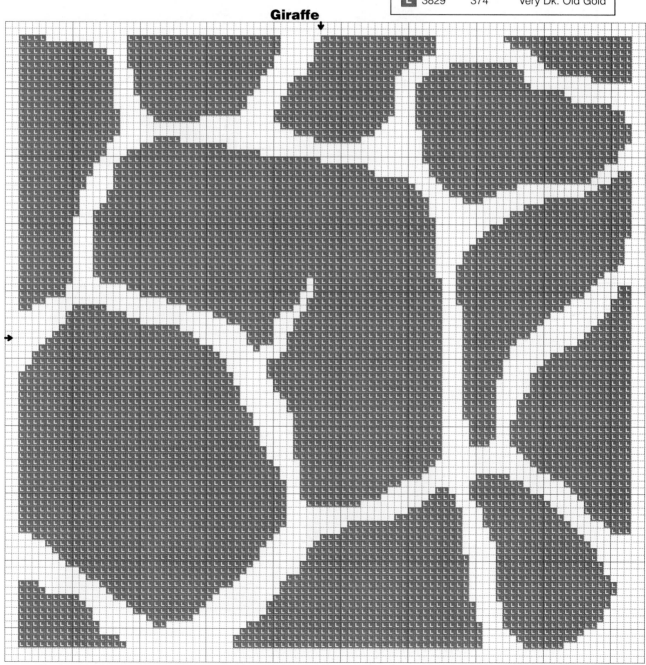

Notes: Trim design to 13½" x 13½" for front. From fabric, cut one 13½" x 13½" piece for back. Use ½" seam allowance.

2: With right sides facing, sew piping to outside edges of front.

3: With right sides facing, sew front and back together, leaving a small opening. Trim seam and turn right sides out; press. Fill with fiberfill; slip stitch opening closed.

**Giraffe Stitch Count:**
91 wide x 91 high

**Approximate Design Size:**
11-count 8⅜" x 8⅜"
14-count 6½" x 6½"
16-count 5¾" x 5¾"
18-count 5⅛" x 5⅛"
22-count 4⅛" x 4⅛"
14-count over two
  threads 13" x 13"

**Zebra Stitch Count:**
98 wide x 98 high

**Approximate Design Size:**
11-count 9" x 9"
14-count 7" x 7"
16-count 6⅛" x 6⅛"
18-count 5½" x 5½"
22-count 4½" x 4½"
14-count over two
  threads 14" x 14"

**Zebra**

| X | DMC® | ANCHOR® | COLORS |
|---|------|---------|--------|
| L | 310  | 403     | Black  |

**Zebra**

# Sampler Address Book

## DESIGNED BY JULIA LUCAS

*W*hat a clever way to organize all of your addresses. You'll want to stitch several for giving to friends and family.

## *Materials*

• Address book with 4½" x 7" white 14-count Vinyl-Weave™ insert

## *Instructions*

Select letters and numbers of choice from Alphabet and Numbers graph for initials and year, center and stitch design, using two strands floss for Cross-Stitch and Backstitch. Assemble address book following manufacturer's instructions.

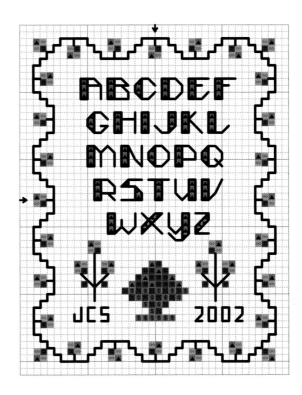

**Alphabet and Numbers**

**Stitch Count:**
36 wide x 48 high

**Approximate Design Size:**
11-count 3⅜" x 4⅜"
14-count 2⅝" x 3½"
16-count 2¼" x 3"
18-count 2" x 2¾"
22-count 1⅝" x 2¼"

| X | B'st | DMC® | ANCHOR® | COLORS |
|---|---|---|---|---|
| ▲ | | 223 | 895 | Lt. Shell Pink |
| ∞ | | 224 | 893 | Very Lt. Shell Pink |
| | ⊟ | 317 | 400 | Pewter Gray |
| ▨ | | 611 | 898 | Drab Brown |
| $ | | 612 | 832 | Lt. Drab Brown |
| ⊞ | | 3815 | 216 | Dk. Celadon Green |

# Watermelon Summer

## DESIGNED BY HOPE MURPHY

Enjoy summer delights all year round with a delicious watermelon basket border and kitchen towel.

## Materials

- Towel with 2½" x 11" seafoam green 14-count Aida insert
- Desired length of 3⅛"-wide Christmas red 16-count Stitchband
- Basket

## Instructions

1: For Towel, center and stitch design onto insert, using three strands floss for Cross-Stitch.

2: For Stitchband, omitting Med. Carnation Cross-Stitch, center and stitch design onto Stitchband, using two strands floss for Cross-Stitch. Position and secure design to basket as shown in photo.

| X | DMC® | ANCHOR® | COLORS |
|---|------|---------|--------|
| ●● | 310 | 403 | Black |
| % | 500 | 683 | Very Dk. Blue Green |
| $ | 504 | 1042 | Very Lt. Blue Green |
| ∞ | 892 | 33 | Med. Carnation |
| ◢ | 3706 | 35 | Med. Melon |

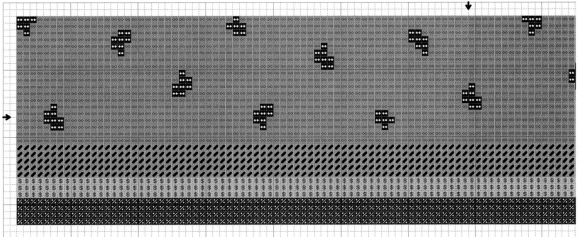

**Stitch Count:**
134 wide x 31 high

**Approximate Design Size:**
11-count 12¼" x 2⅞"
14-count 9⅝" x 2¼"
16-count 8⅜" x 2"
18-count 7½" x 1¾"
22-count 6⅛" x 1½"

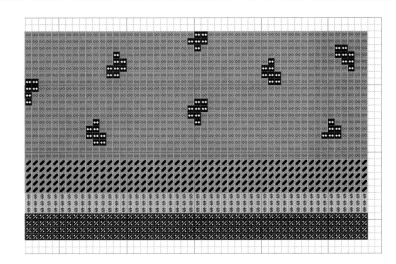

*101 Quick & Easy Cross-Stitch Projects*

# Hearts and Flowers

## DESIGNED BY MARY B. JONES

*S*pecialty stitches and variegated threads combine to create this unique design.

## Materials

- 9" x 9" piece of lambs-wool 10-count Betsy Ross Linen
- Wooden box with 6" x 6" design opening
- 1" heart button

## Instructions

Center and stitch design, using one strand floss for Cross-Stitch, Running Stitch, Rhodes Heart and Modified Waffle Stitch. Use six strands coordinating floss for securing button. Position and secure design in box following manufacturer's instructions.

**Stitch Count:**
48 wide x 48 high

**Approximate Design Size:**
11-count 4³⁄₈" x 4³⁄₈"
14-count 3¹⁄₂" x 3¹⁄₂"
16-count 3" x 3"
18-count 2³⁄₄" x 2³⁄₄"
22-count 2¹⁄₄" x 2¹⁄₄"

**Modified Waffle Stitch**

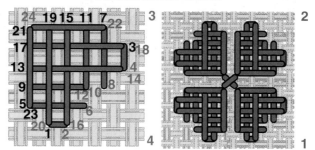

Follow numbering sequence for first petal; rotate ¹⁄₄" turn around center Cross Stitch; stitch second petal. Repeat for third and fourth petals.

| X | Run | Rhm | ModW | CARON WATERCOLORS | COLORS |
|---|-----|-----|------|-------------------|--------|
| $ | ▭ | ▭ | ▭ | 93 | Painted Desert |

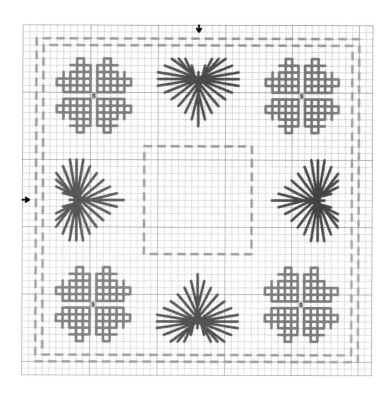

# Stenciled Bouquet

## DESIGNED BY BARBARA SESTOK

Capture the elegance of stenciling with this glorious fresh bouquet.

## Materials

- 13" x 13" piece of white 28-count Meran
- 1½ yds. fabric
- 2 yds. lace
- 14" x 14" pillow form

## Instructions

1: Center and stitch design, stitching over two threads and using two strands floss for Cross-Stitch and one strand floss for Backstitch.

Notes: Trim design to 10" x 10". From fabric, cut two 3¾" x 10" for A pieces, two 3¾" x 15½" for B pieces and two 10½" x 15½" pieces for back. Use ½" seam allowance.

2: With right sides facing, sew design, A and B pieces together according to Front Assembly Diagram, forming front.

3: With right sides facing, sew lace to front.

4: Hem one 15½" edge of each back piece. Place one hemmed edge over the other, overlapping enough to create a 15½" x 15½" back with opening. Baste outside edges together; press.

5: With right sides facing, sew front and back together. Trim seam and turn right sides out; press. Insert pillow form.

**Front Assembly Diagram**

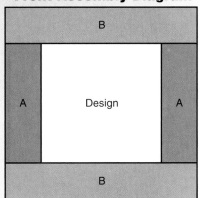

| X | B'st | DMC® | ANCHOR® | COLORS |
|---|------|------|---------|--------|
| ▼ | | 208 | 110 | Very Dk. Lavender |
| − | | 209 | 109 | Dk. Lavender |
| ↑ | | 561 | 212 | Very Dk. Jade |
| △ | | 562 | 210 | Med. Jade |
| ∴ | | 563 | 208 | Lt. Jade |
| + | | 3340 | 329 | Med. Apricot |
| ✦ | | 3341 | 328 | Apricot |
| ▦ | | 3350 | 59 | Ultra Dk. Dusty Rose |
| ★ | | 3731 | 76 | Very Dk. Dusty Rose |
| ∴ | | 3733 | 75 | Dusty Rose |
| | − | 3799 | 236 | Very Dk. Pewter Gray |
| ○ | | 3820 | 306 | Dk. Straw |
| ✳ | | 3824 | 8 | Lt. Apricot |
| $ | | 3838 | 146 | Dk. Lavender Blue |
| ⁒ | | 3839 | 145 | Med. Lavender Blue |

**Stitch Count:**
100 wide x 100 high

**Approximate Design Size:**
11-count 9⅛" x 9⅛"
14-count 7¼" x 7¼"
16-count 6¼" x 6¼"
18-count 5⅝" x 5⅝"
22-count 4⅝" x 4⅝"
28-count over two
  threads 7¼" x 7¼"

# Feathered Family

## DESIGNED BY RONDA BRYCE

*I*f you love roosters and
chickens, this set is for
you. This feathered
family will brighten
your kitchen decor.

## Materials

• One 9" x 9" piece
(for Notepad Holder)
and one 10" x 12" piece
(for Recipe Box) of white
11-count Aida
• Wooden notepad holder
with 4" x 4" design opening
• Wooden recipe box
with 4" x 6" design opening

## Instructions

1: For Notepad Holder,
center and stitch "Heart
and Rooster" design onto
9" x 9" piece of Aida,
using four strands floss
for Cross-Stitch and
two strands floss for
Backstitch and French
Knot. Position and secure
design in notepad holder
following manufacturer's
instructions.

2: For Recipe Box,
center and stitch "Heart
and Hen" design onto 10"
x 12" piece of Aida,
using four strands floss
for Cross-Stitch and
two strands floss for
Backstitch and French
Knot. Position and secure
design in recipe box
following manufacturer's
instructions.

**Heart and Hen
Stitch Count:**
54 wide x 40 high

**Approximate
Design Size:**
11-count 5" x 3⅝"
14-count 3⅞" x 2⅞"
16-count 3⅜" x 2½"
18-count 3" x 2¼"
22-count 2½" x 1⅞"

### Heart and Hen

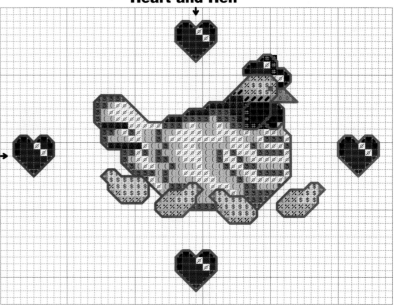

### Heart and Hen

| X | B'st | Fr | DMC® | ANCHOR® | COLORS |
|---|---|---|---|---|---|
| ⊟ | | ● | 310 | 403 | Black |
| 3 | | | 318 | 399 | Lt. Steel Gray |
| ■ | | | 321 | 9046 | Red |
| ◮ | | | 414 | 235 | Dk. Steel Gray |
| $ | | | 445 | 288 | Lt. Lemon |
| ■ | | | 498 | 1005 | Dk. Red |
| ○ | | | 741 | 304 | Med. Tangerine |
| ⬤ | | | 742 | 303 | Lt. Tangerine |
| ( | | | 762 | 234 | Very Lt. Pearl Gray |
| # | | | 814 | 45 | Dk. Garnet |
| % | | | 973 | 297 | Bright Canary |
| ∅ | | | White | 2 | White |

## Heart and Rooster

| X | B'st | Fr | DMC® | ANCHOR® | COLORS |
|---|------|-----|------|---------|--------|
| | ⊟ | ⬤ | 310 | 403 | Black |
| | | | 321 | 9046 | Red |
| | | | 414 | 235 | Dk. Steel Gray |
| ★ | | | 433 | 358 | Med. Brown |
| | | | 435 | 1046 | Very Lt. Brown |
| $ | | | 445 | 288 | Lt. Lemon |
| | | | 498 | 1005 | Dk. Red |
| ◊ | | | 741 | 301 | Med. Tangerine |
| | | | 742 | 303 | Lt. Tangerine |
| ( | | | 762 | 234 | Very Lt. Pearl Gray |
| # | | | 814 | 45 | Dk. Garnet |
| ○ | | | 898 | 360 | Very Dk. Coffee Brown |
| % | | | 973 | 297 | Bright Canary |
| — | | | 991 | 189 | Dk. Aquamarine |
| ♦ | | | 992 | 187 | Lt. Aquamarine |
| + | | | 3813 | 213 | Lt. Blue Green |
| ∅ | | | White | 2 | White |

## Heart and Rooster

**Heart and Rooster Stitch Count:**
36 wide x 39 high

**Approximate Design Size:**
11-count 3⅜" x 3⅝"
14-count 2⅝" x 2⅞"
16-count 2¼" x 2½"
18-count 2" x 2¼"
22-count 1⅝" x 1⅞"

# Floral Essence

## DESIGNED BY LOIS WINSTON

This graceful table topper brings a sophisticated note of freshness to any setting.

## Materials

• 36" x 36" piece of cream 14-count Lincoln
• 4½ yds. flat lace

## Instructions

1: Center and stitch design onto each corner, beginning 2½" from outside edges, using two strands floss for Cross-Stitch and Backstitch.

2: Press under a ½" hem on edges; sew lace around front outside edges, mitering corners as you sew.

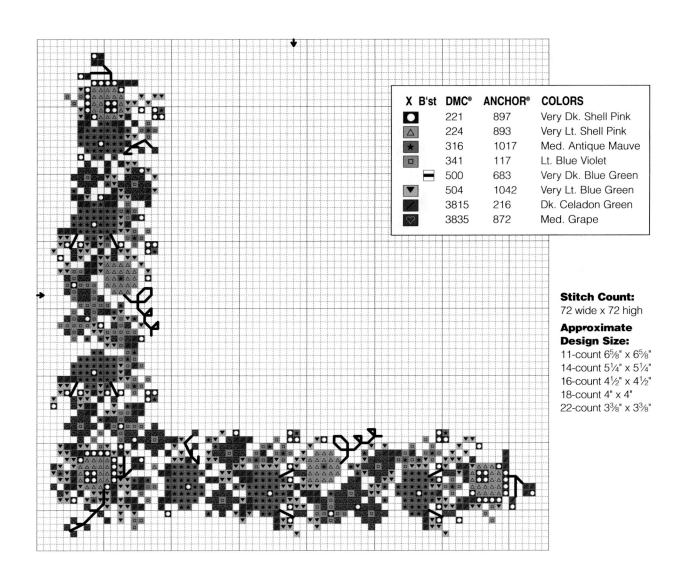

| X | B'st | DMC® | ANCHOR® | COLORS |
|---|------|------|---------|--------|
| ● | | 221 | 897 | Very Dk. Shell Pink |
| △ | | 224 | 893 | Very Lt. Shell Pink |
| ★ | | 316 | 1017 | Med. Antique Mauve |
| ▫ | | 341 | 117 | Lt. Blue Violet |
| | ▬ | 500 | 683 | Very Dk. Blue Green |
| ▼ | | 504 | 1042 | Very Lt. Blue Green |
| ◹ | | 3815 | 216 | Dk. Celadon Green |
| ♡ | | 3835 | 872 | Med. Grape |

**Stitch Count:**
72 wide x 72 high

**Approximate Design Size:**
11-count 6⅝" x 6⅝"
14-count 5¼" x 5¼"
16-count 4½" x 4½"
18-count 4" x 4"
22-count 3⅜" x 3⅜"

# Hummingbird Coasters

## DESIGNED BY MIKE VICKERY

**B**right and colorful hummingbirds remind us of the wonder of spring.

## Materials for One

• 9" x 9" piece of white 14-count Aida
• Acrylic coaster with 3"-round design opening

## Instructions

Center and stitch design of choice, using two strands floss for Cross-Stitch and one strand floss for Backstitch. Position and secure design in coaster following manufacturer's instructions.

**Purple**
**Stitch Count:**
35 wide x 29 high

**Approximate Design Size:**
11-count 3¼" x 2⅝"
14-count 2½" x 2⅛"
16-count 2¼" x 1⅞"
18-count 2" x 1⅝"
22-count 1⅝" x 1⅜"

**Yellow**
**Stitch Count:**
40 wide x 29 high

**Approximate Design Size:**
11-count 3⅝" x 2⅝"
14-count 2⅞" x 2⅛"
16-count 2½" x 1⅞"
18-count 2¼" x 1⅝"
22-count 1⅞" x 1⅜"

**Green**
**Stitch Count:**
30 wide x 29 high

**Approximate Design Size:**
11-count 2¾" x 2⅝"
14-count 2¼" x 2⅛"
16-count 1⅞" x 1⅞"
18-count 1¾" x 1⅝"
22-count 1⅜" x 1⅜"

**Blue**
**Stitch Count:**
36 wide x 28 high

**Approximate Design Size:**
11-count 3⅜" x 2⅝"
14-count 2⅝" x 2"
16-count 2¼" x 1¾"
18-count 2" x 1⅝"
22-count 1⅝" x 1⅜"

## Yellow

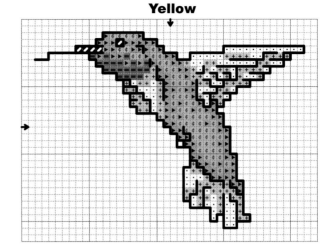

## Blue

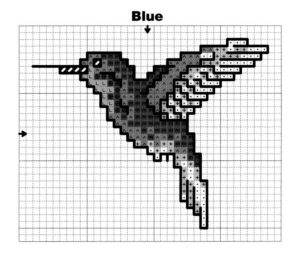

## Green

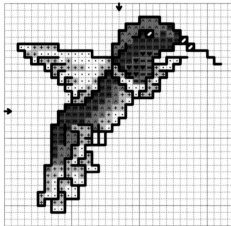

## Purple

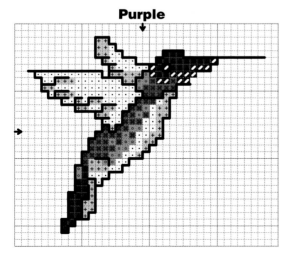

| X | B'st | DMC® | ANCHOR® | COLORS |
|---|---|---|---|---|
| ⌘ | | 208 | 110 | Very Dk. Lavender |
| o | | 210 | 108 | Med. Lavender |
| ◩ | | 310 | 403 | Black |
| ⊕ | | 334 | 977 | Med. Baby Blue |
| ♥ | | 349 | 13 | Dk. Coral |
| = | | 351 | 10 | Coral |
| ■ | | 413 | 104 | Dk. Pewter Gray |
| + | | 822 | 390 | Lt. Beige Gray |
| m | | 912 | 209 | Lt. Emerald Green |
| ^ | | 954 | 203 | Nile Green |
| L | | 3325 | 129 | Lt. Baby Blue |
| | ▬ | 3799 | 236 | Very Dk. Pewter Gray |
| ▶ | | 3820 | 306 | Dk. Straw |
| ¢ | | 3822 | 295 | Lt. Straw |
| · | | White | 2 | White |

# Fleurs-de-lys

## DESIGNED BY MIKE VICKERY

**T**ired of the
cumbersome and
messy job of bringing
in the firewood?
Bring to life a handy,
stylish log tote with a
regal border design.

## Materials

• 12" x 16" piece of
10-count Waste Canvas
• Two 4" x 23" pieces
and two 18" x 28" pieces
of canvas

## Instructions

1: For Log Carrier front,
center and apply waste
canvas 5¼" from one
short edge on one
18" x 28" piece of canvas,
following manufacturer's
instructions. Center
and stitch design,
using six strands floss
for Cross-Stitch and
two strands floss for
Backstitch. Remove waste
canvas after stitching
following manufacturer's
instructions.

2: For handles, with
right sides facing, fold
each 4" x 23" piece in half
lengthwise; sew long
edges together. Turn right
sides out; press. With right
sides facing, position
unfinished edges of each
handle to each end of
front; baste.

3: With right sides
facing, sew front and
remaining 18" x 28" piece
of canvas together, leaving
an opening for turning.
Turn right sides out; slip
stitch opening closed.

**Stitch Count:**
100 wide x 58 high

**Approximate
Design Size:**
10-count 10" x 6"
11-count 9⅛" x 5⅜"
14-count 7¼" x 4¼"
16-count 6¼" x 3¾"
18-count 5⅝" x 3¼"
22-count 4⅝" x 2¾"

| X | B'st | DMC® | ANCHOR® | COLORS |
|---|---|---|---|---|
| 8 | | 334 | 977 | Med. Baby Blue |
| ▲ | | 336 | 150 | Navy Blue |
| ♥ | | 498 | 1065 | Dk. Red |
| S | | 676 | 891 | Lt. Old Gold |
| L | | 3325 | 129 | Lt. Baby Blue |
| ⊟ | | 3799 | 236 | Very Dk. Pewter Gray |

# Bathroom Fishies

## DESIGNED BY MIKE VICKERY

**E**xperience the color and wonder of the undersea world. Mornings will be brighter when you have this fun toothbrush caddy, soap dispenser and tiebacks to help start the day.

Caddy, center and stitch "Orange Fish" design onto Vinyl-Aida insert, using two strands floss for Cross-Stitch and one strand floss for Backstitch. Assemble caddy following manufacturer's instructions.

Note: To make right and left tieback, stitch one design on each piece of Stitchband on opposite ends.

3: For Tiebacks, beginning 9" from one short end, center and stitch "Fish School"

## Materials

- Dispenser with white 14-count Vinyl-Weave™ insert
- Toothbrush caddy with white 14-count Vinyl-Weave™ insert
- Two 18" pieces of light blue/antique white 3.1"-wide 27-count Celeste Stitchband
- Two ½" plastic rings
- Two Velcro® fasteners

## Instructions

1: For Dispenser, center and stitch "Yellow Fish" design onto Vinyl-Aida insert, using two strands floss for Cross-Stitch and one strand floss for Backstitch. Assemble dispenser following manufacturer's instructions.

2: For Toothbrush

### Orange Fish

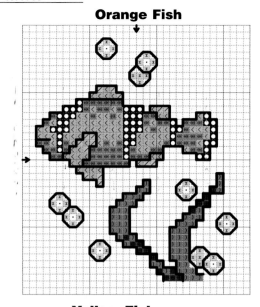

design onto each 18" piece of Stitchband, stitching over two threads and using two strands floss for Cross-Stitch and one strand floss for Backstitch.

4: Hem short ends of each tieback. Tack plastic ring to tieback at opposite end of design. Stitch Velcro® to wrong sides at short ends.

**Orange Fish Stitch Count:**
30 wide x 36 high

**Approximate Design Size:**
11-count 2¾" x 3⅜"
14-count 2¼" x 2⅝"
16-count 1⅞" x 2¼"
18-count 1¾" x 2"
22-count 1⅜" x 1⅝"

| X | B'st | DMC® | ANCHOR® | COLORS |
|---|------|------|---------|--------|
| ⬤ | | 310 | 403 | Black |
| ⧀ | | 721 | 324 | Med. Orange Spice |
| Y | | 725 | 305 | Topaz |
| L | | 727 | 293 | Very Lt. Topaz |
| ╱ | | 762 | 234 | Very Lt. Pearl Gray |
| I | | 775 | 128 | Very Lt. Baby Blue |
| ⊕ | | 910 | 229 | Dk. Emerald Green |
| ) | | 913 | 204 | Med. Nile Green |
| | ▬ | 3799 | 236 | Very Dk. Pewter Gray |
| < | | 3825 | 323 | Pale Pumpkin |
| · | | White | 2 | White |

**Fish School Stitch Count:**
84 wide x 27 high

**Approximate Design Size:**
11-count 7⅝" x 2½"
14-count 6" x 2"
16-count 5¼" x 1¾"
18-count 4¾" x 1½"
22-count 3⅞" x 1¼"
27-count over two threads 6¼" x 2"

**Yellow Fish Stitch Count:**
38 wide x 38 high

**Approximate Design Size:**
11-count 3½" x 3½"
14-count 2¾" x 2¾"
16-count 2⅜" x 2⅜"
18-count 2⅛" x 2⅛"
22-count 1¾" x 1¾"

### Yellow Fish

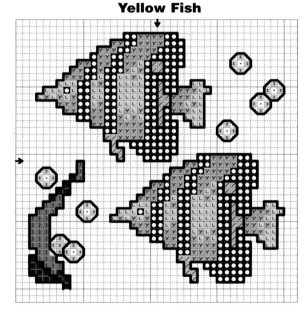

### Fish School

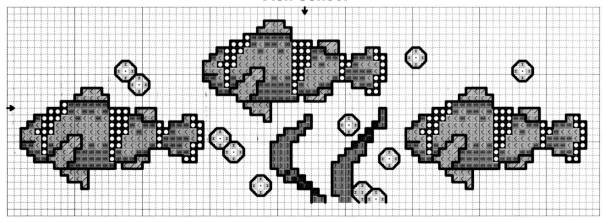

# Celestial Dreams

## DESIGNED BY MIKE VICKERY

**B**ring the essence of the celestial bodies right into your favorite room with this mystical pillow sham.

## Materials

- 26" x 32½" piece of navy 10-count Tula
- ¾ yd. fabric
- Standard bed pillow

## Instructions

1: Center and stitch design, stitching over two threads and using two strands perle coton for Cross-Stitch and one strand perle cotton for Backstitch.

Notes: From fabric, cut two 18½" x 26" pieces for back. Use ½" seam allowance.

2: Hem one 26" edge of each back piece. Place one hemmed edge over the other, overlapping enough to create a 26" x 32½" back with opening. Baste outside edges together; press.

3: For Pillow Sham, with right sides facing, sew design and back together. Trim seam and turn right sides out; press. To form pillow sham pocket, topstitch 2¼" from outside edges.

**Stitch Count:**
100 wide x 80 high

**Approximate Design Size:**
11-count 9⅛" x 7⅜"
14-count 7¼" x 5¾"
16-count 6¼" x 5"
18-count 5⅝" x 4½"
22-count 4⅝" x 3⅝"
10-count over two
  threads 20" x 16"

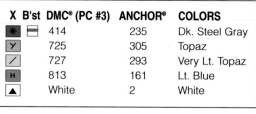

| X | B'st | DMC® (PC #3) | ANCHOR® | COLORS |
|---|------|--------------|---------|--------|
| ✳ | ▭ | 414 | 235 | Dk. Steel Gray |
| Y | | 725 | 305 | Topaz |
| ╱ | | 727 | 293 | Very Lt. Topaz |
| H | | 813 | 161 | Lt. Blue |
| ▲ | | White | 2 | White |

# Spectator Sports

### DESIGNED BY MIKE VICKERY

**Football**

**Basketball**

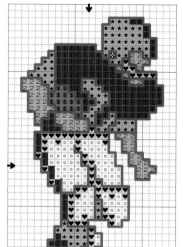

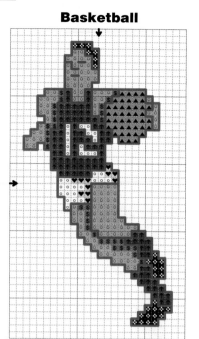

*S*ports enthusiasts will love this afghan! It's perfect to cuddle up with as you watch the big game.

## Materials

• 54" x 54" piece of blue/beige 14-count Hearthside® afghan fabric

## Instructions

Center and stitch one design onto each afghan panel following Stitching Diagram, using six strands floss for Cross-Stitch and two strands floss for Backstitch. Hem edges of afghan, mitering corners as you sew.

**Stitching Diagram**

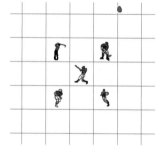

*101 Quick & Easy Cross-Stitch Projects*

# Spectator Sports

**Football**
**Stitch Count:**
21 wide x 44 high
**Approximate Design Size:**
11-count 2" x 4"
14-count 1½" x 3¼"
16-count 1⅜" x 2¾"
18-count 1¼" x 2½"
22-count 1" x 2"
14-count over two
 threads 3" x 6⅜"

**Basketball**
**Stitch Count:**
22 wide x 42 high
**Approximate Design Size:**
11-count 2" x 3⅞"
14-count 1⅝" x 3"
16-count 1⅜" x 2⅝"
18-count 1¼" x 2⅜"
22-count 1" x 2"
14-count over two
 threads 3¼" x 6"

**Hockey**
**Stitch Count:**
28 wide x 46 high
**Approximate Design Size:**
11-count 2⅝" x 4¼"
14-count 2" x 3⅜"
16-count 1¾" x 2⅞"
18-count 1⅝" x 2⅝"
22-count 1⅜" x 2⅛"
14-count over two
 threads 4" x 6⅝"

**Baseball**
**Stitch Count:**
33 wide x 46 high
**Approximate Design Size:**
11-count 3" x 4¼"
14-count 2⅜" x 3⅜"
16-count 2⅛" x 2⅞"
18-count 1⅞" x 2⅝"
22-count 1½" x 2⅛"
14-count over two
 threads 4¾" x 6⅝"

**Golf**
**Stitch Count:**
29 wide x 43 high
**Approximate Design Size:**
11-count 2⅝" x 4"
14-count 2⅛" x 3⅛"
16-count 1⅞" x 2¾"
18-count 1⅝" x 2⅜"
22-count 1⅜" x 2"
14-count over two
 threads 4¼" x 6¼"

## Hockey
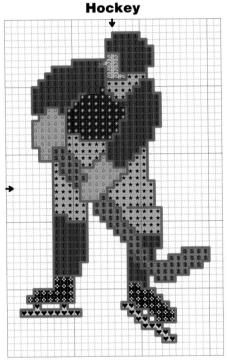

## Baseball

## Golf
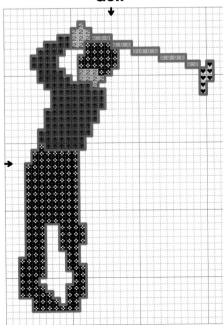

| X | B'st | DMC® | ANCHOR® | COLORS |
|---|---|---|---|---|
| ❖ | | 310 | 403 | Black |
| # | | 350 | 11 | Med. Coral |
| $ | | 436 | 1045 | Tan |
| ★ | | 676 | 891 | Lt. Old Gold |
| ▲ | | 722 | 323 | Lt. Orange Spice |
| ◊ | | 738 | 361 | Very Lt. Tan |
| ◖ | | 798 | 131 | Dk. Delft Blue |
| ◢ | | 817 | 13 | Very Dk. Coral Red |
| ✳ | | 820 | 134 | Very Dk. Royal Blue |
| ♥ | | 822 | 390 | Lt. Beige Gray |
| ↑ | | 911 | 205 | Med. Emerald Green |
| 2 | | 945 | 881 | Tawny |
| | ▬ | 3799 | 236 | Very Dk. Pewter Gray |
| ○ | | White | 2 | White |

# Lighthouses

## DESIGNED BY JULIA LUCAS

*P*erfect for any den, office or any nautical nook. Imagine rounding the point to see either of these majestic lighthouses showing the way clear.

## Materials for One

• 8" x 9" piece of forget-me-not-blue 14-count Aida

## Instructions

Center and stitch design of choice, using two strands floss for Cross-Stitch and one strand floss for Backstitch.

**Red Lighthouse Stitch Count:**
30 wide x 39 high

**Approximate Design Size:**
11-count 2¾" x 3⅝"
14-count 2¼" x 2⅞"
16-count 1⅞" x 2½"
18-count 1¾" x 2¼"
22-count 1⅜" x 1⅞"

**White Lighthouse Stitch Count:**
30 wide x 37 high

**Approximate Design Size:**
11-count 2¾" x 3⅜"
14-count 2¼" x 2¾"
16-count 1⅞" x 2⅜"
18-count 1¾" x 2⅛"
22-count 1⅜" x 1¾"

| X | B'st | DMC® | ANCHOR® | COLORS |
|---|---|---|---|---|
| ◩ | ▭ | 310 | 403 | Black |
| 2 | | 318 | 399 | Lt. Steel Gray |
| ✳ | | 320 | 215 | Med. Pistachio Green |
| ⊞ | | 322 | 978 | Dk. Baby Blue |
| ⊠ | | 350 | 11 | Med. Coral |
| ⊡ | ▭ | 414 | 235 | Dk. Steel Gray |
| $ | | 415 | 398 | Pearl Gray |
| ◼ | | 611 | 898 | Drab Brown |
| ( | | 613 | 831 | Very Lt. Drab Brown |
| ▲ | | 817 | 13 | Very Dk. Coral Red |
| # | | White | 2 | White |

**Red Lighthouse**

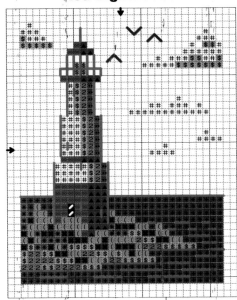

**White Lighthouse**

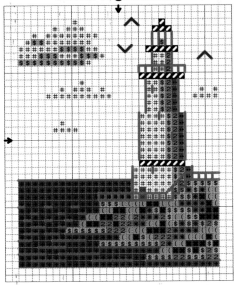

# Welcome Irises

## DESIGNED BY PATRICIA MALONEY MARTIN

**B**id guests a warm welcome with this quick-to-stitch timeless design.

## Materials

• 11" x 13" piece of potato 25-count Lugana®
• Wooden clock with 7" x 9" design opening

## Instructions

Center and stitch design, stitching over two threads and using three strands floss for Cross-Stitch and Backstitch of lettering. Use two strands floss for Backstitch of stamens. Use two strands floss for French Knot. Use one strand floss for remaining Backstitch. Assemble clock following manufacturer's instructions.

**Stitch Count:**
60 wide x 85 high

**Approximate Design Size:**
11-count 5½" x 7¾"
14-count 4⅜" x 6⅛"
16-count 3¾" x 5⅜"
18-count 3⅜" x 4¾"
22-count 2¾" x 3⅞"
25-count over two
 threads 4⅞" x 6⅞"

| X | B'st | Fr | DMC® | ANCHOR® | COLORS |
|---|------|----|------|---------|--------|
| ▲ | | | 208 | 110 | Very Dk. Lavender |
| # | | | 210 | 108 | Med. Lavender |
| | ▭ | | 310 | 403 | Black |
| · | ▭ | | 444 | 290 | Dk. Lemon |
| 2 | | | 702 | 226 | Kelly Green |
| ✓ | | ● | 741 | 304 | Med. Tangerine |
| ◌ | | | 815 | 43 | Med. Garnet |
| ★ | ▭ | ● | 890 | 218 | Ultra Dk. Pistachio Green |
| ♥ | | | 3687 | 68 | Mauve |
| ∞ | | | 3689 | 49 | Lt. Mauve |

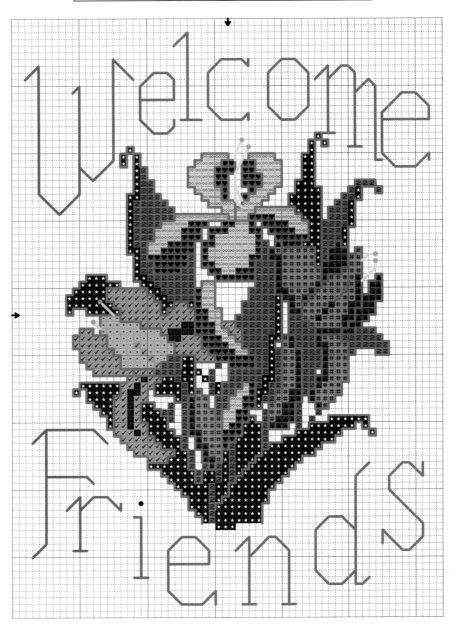

# Safari Powder Puffs
## DESIGNED BY SHARON MOONEY

*Exciting animal print borders add that extra flair to your boudoir.*

## Materials for One

- 7" x 10" piece of white 14-count Aida
- ¼ yd. faux fur

## Instructions

1: Center and stitch design of choice, using two strands floss for Cross-Stitch.

Notes: Trim design to 1¾" x 4½". From faux fur, cut two according to Powder Puff Pattern for front and back. Use ¼" seam allowance.

2: Press under long edges of design; slip stitch in place. Center wrong side of design on right side of front, baste short edges in place. With right sides facing, sew front and back together, leaving a small opening for turning. Turn right sides out; slip stitch opening closed.

**Tiger, Leopard, Zebra and Giraffe Stitch Count:**
55 wide x 10 high

**Approximate Design Size:**
11-count 5" x 1"
14-count 4" x ¾"
16-count 3½" x ⅝"
18-count 3⅛" x ⅝"
22-count 2½" x ½"

Safari Powder Puffs

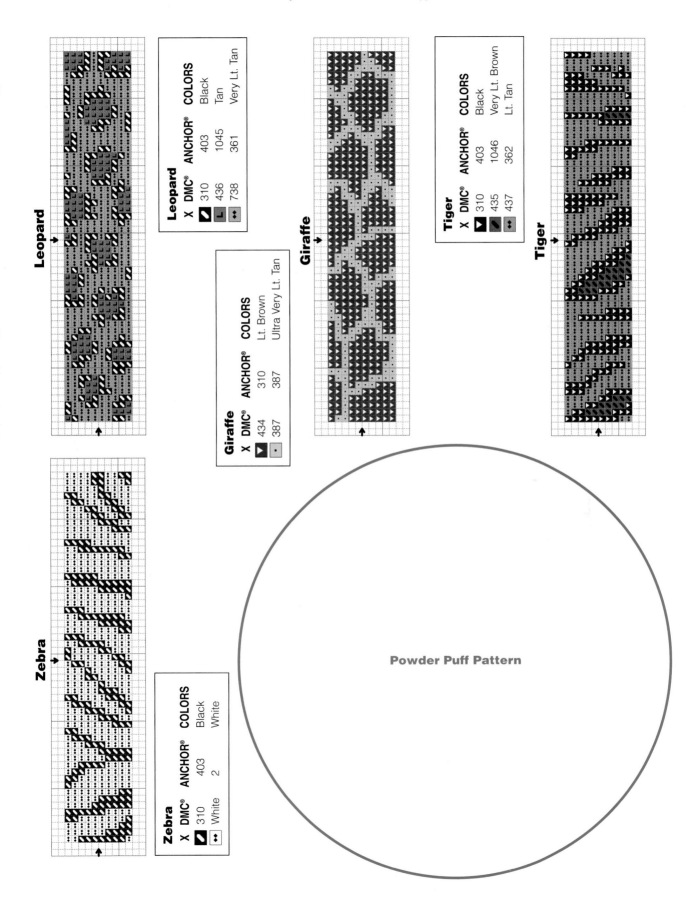

# Chapter Two

# Fabulous Fashions

From casual to elegant, you can choose from a host of fashionable accessories on the following pages. There are so many opportunities and occasions to wear these creations or give them as gifts. It's always exciting to wear a new piece of clothing and become the focus of everyone's attention. It's great to be able to say that "I made it myself," and bask in the glow of admiring comments.

# Handy Totes

## DESIGNED BY HOPE MURPHY

*Get ready for compliments when you carry these clever tote bags. Admirers will be asking where you got them, and you'll feel great saying, "I stitched them myself!"*

## Materials for One

- 15" x 25" Huck Showcase Towel with 4½" x 6" ecru 14-count Aida insert
- ¼ yd. lining fabric
- Interfacing
- 1 yd. 1¼" webbing
- Two decorative buttons

## Instructions

Notes: For "Teacher," select letters of choice for name from Alphabet graph.

1: Center and stitch design of choice onto insert following Babykins Stitching Diagram (see page 172), using three strands floss for Cross-Stitch and two strands floss for Backstitch.

Notes: From lining fabric and interfacing, cut one each 15" x 25". Use ½" seam allowance.

2: For lining, apply interfacing to wrong side of lining fabric following manufacturer's instructions.

3: For handles, cut webbing in half. Position one handle to wrong side of each short edge on towel; secure in place.

4: With right sides facing, sew towel and lining together, leaving an opening for turning. Turn right sides out; slip stitch opening closed.

5: With right sides facing and matching short edges, sew towel together at sides, forming tote. Turn right sides out.

6: Sew buttons to front of tote as shown in photo.

**Beach Babe**

| X | B'st | DMC® | ANCHOR® | COLORS |
|---|---|---|---|---|
| ◊ | ▭ | 333 | 119 | Very Dk. Blue Violet |
|  | ▭ | 340 | 118 | Med. Blue Violet |
| % |  | 666 | 46 | Bright Red |
| ◆◆ |  | 726 | 295 | Lt. Topaz |
| •• |  | 891 | 35 | Dk. Carnation |
| ( | ▭ | 900 | 333 | Dk. Burnt Orange |
| # |  | 970 | 316 | Lt. Pumpkin |
| $ |  | 972 | 298 | Deep Canary |
| ∞ |  | 996 | 433 | Med. Electric Blue |
| ) |  | White | 2 | White |

**Beach Babe**

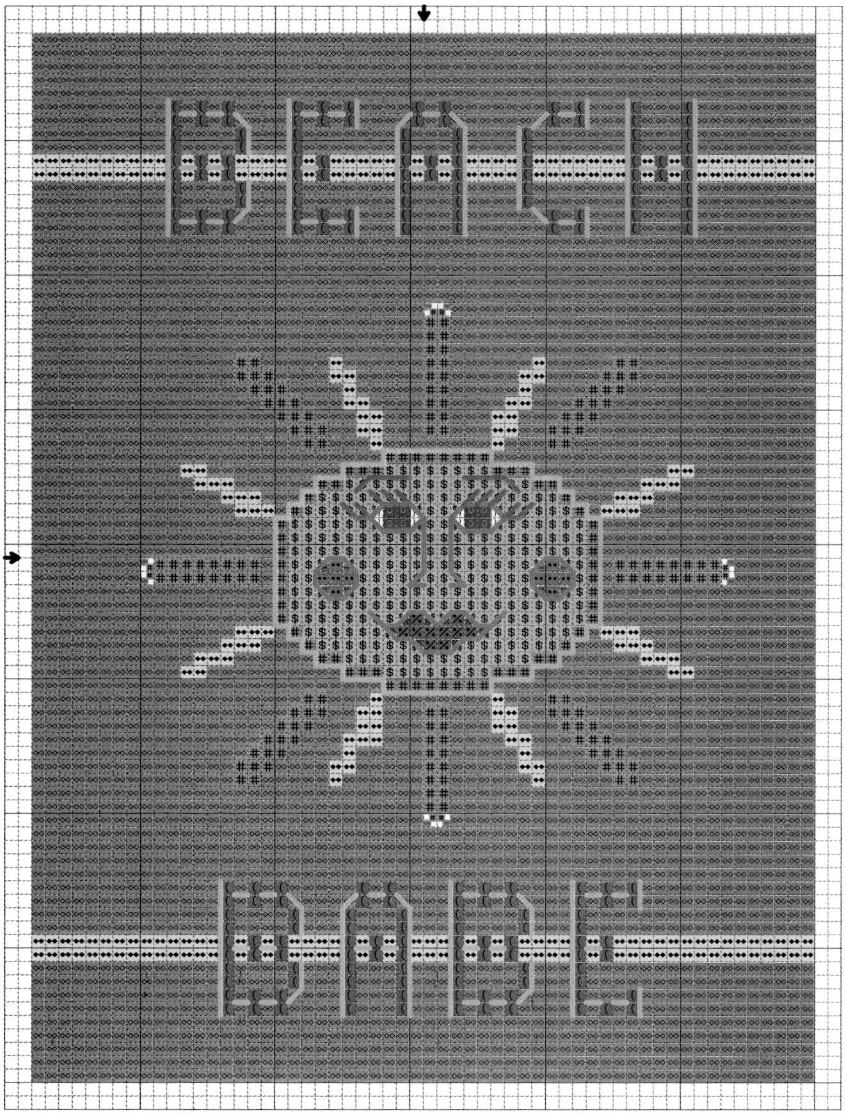

**Beach Babe Stitch Count:**
58 wide x 78 high

**Approximate Design Size:**
11-count 5⅜" x 7⅛"
14-count 4¼" x 5⅝"
16-count 3⅝" x 4⅞"
18-count 3¼" x 4⅜"
22-count 2⅝" x 3⅝"

*101 Quick & Easy Cross-Stitch Projects*

**Teacher**

**Teacher
Stitch Count:**
56 wide x 76 high

**Approximate
Design Size:**
11-count 5⅛" x 7"
14-count 4" x 5½"
16-count 3½" x 4¾"
18-count 3⅛" x 4¼"
22-count 2⅝" x 3½"

| X | B'st | DMC® | ANCHOR® | COLORS |
|---|---|---|---|---|
| ( | | 318 | 399 | Lt. Steel Gray |
| ▲ | ▬ | 321 | 9046 | Red |
| $ | | 326 | 59 | Very Dk. Rose |
| # | ▭ | 762 | 234 | Very Lt. Pearl Gray |
| + | | 820 | 134 | Very Dk. Royal Blue |
| $ | | 841 | 378 | Lt. Beige Brown |
| ↑ | | 898 | 360 | Very Dk. Coffee Brown |
| ) | ▬ | 3799 | 236 | Very Dk. Pewter Gray |
| O | | Ecru | 387 | Ecru |
| * | | White | 2 | White |

**Alphabet**

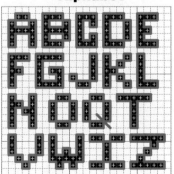

# Snowman Minis

## DESIGNED BY JACQUELYN FOX

*These cheerful snow-men know what it takes to add fun to winter days. Embellish a headband, socks or other accessories with these delightful motifs.*

## Materials

- Knit headband
- Pair of socks
- Five 3" x 2½" pieces of 14-count waste canvas
- Interfacing

## Instructions

1: For Headband, position and baste interfacing to wrong side of headband where motifs are desired; next apply three pieces of waste canvas to right side of headband over interfacing following manufacturer's instructions. Center and stitch designs of choice, using two strands floss for Cross-Stitch and one strand floss for Backstitch.

2: For each Sock, position and baste interfacing to wrong side of sock where motif is desired; next apply one piece of waste canvas to right side of sock over interfacing following manufacturer's instructions. Center and stitch design of choice, using two strands floss for Cross-Stitch and one strand floss for Backstitch.

3: Remove waste canvas after stitching following manufacturer's instructions. Trim interfacing close to stitching.

**Bird**

**Bird
Stitch Count:**
25 wide x 25 high

**Approximate
Design Size:**
11-count 2⅜" x 2⅜"
14-count 1⅞" x 1⅞"
16-count 1⅝" x 1⅝"
18-count 1⅜" x 1⅜"
22-count 1⅛" x 1⅛"

| X | B'st | DMC® | ANCHOR® | COLORS |
|---|------|------|---------|--------|
| + | ▬ | 310 | 403 | Black |
| ✖ | ▬ | 318 | 399 | Lt. Steel Gray |
| # | | 561 | 212 | Very Dk. Jade |
| $ | | 562 | 210 | Med. Jade |
| % | | 563 | 208 | Lt. Jade |
| 3 | | 666 | 46 | Bright Red |
| ✳ | | 760 | 1022 | Salmon |
| ( | | 816 | 20 | Garnet |
| ▼ | | 822 | 390 | Lt. Beige Gray |
| ✱ | | 844 | 1041 | Ultra Dk. Beaver Gray |
| T | | 922 | 1003 | Lt. Copper |
| ↑ | | 930 | 1035 | Dk. Antique Blue |
| ☆ | | 931 | 1034 | Med. Antique Blue |
| ● | | 3752 | 1032 | Very Lt. Antique Blue |
| / | | 3822 | 295 | Lt. Straw |
| 7 | | 3852 | 307 | Very Dk. Straw |
| n | | White | 2 | White |

## Happy

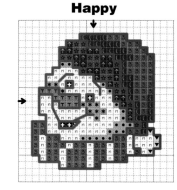

**Happy
Stitch Count:**
19 wide x 20 high

**Approximate
Design Size:**
11-count 1¾" x 1⅞"
14-count 1⅜" x 1½"
16-count 1¼" x 1¼"
18-count 1⅛" x 1⅛"
22-count 1" x 1"

## Skater

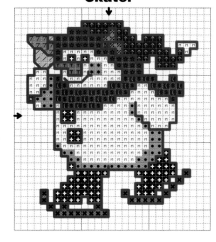

**Skater
Stitch Count:**
25 wide x 29 high

**Approximate
Design Size:**
11-count 2⅜" x 2⅝"
14-count 1⅞" x 2⅛"
16-count 1⅝" x 1⅞"
18-count 1⅜" x 1⅝"
22-count 1⅛" x 1⅜"

## Caroler

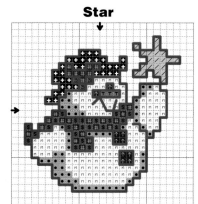

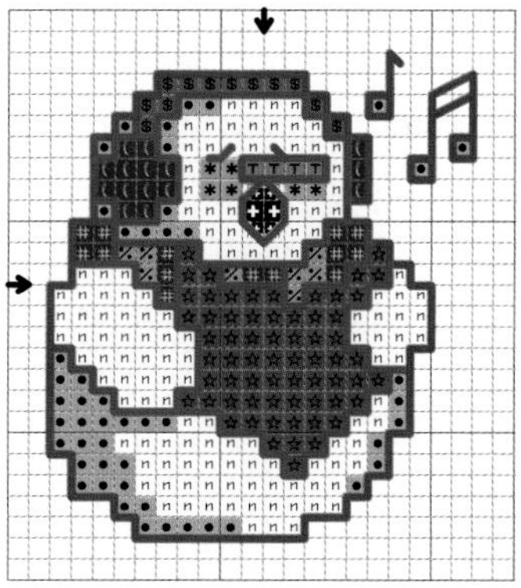

**Caroler
Stitch Count:**
20 wide x 23 high

**Approximate
Design Size:**
11-count 1⅞" x 2⅛"
14-count 1½" x 1¾"
16-count 1¼" x 1½"
18-count 1⅛" x 1⅜"
22-count 1" x 1⅛"

## Star

**Star
Stitch Count:**
23 wide x 23 high

**Approximate
Design Size:**
11-count 2⅛" x 2⅛"
14-count 1¾" x 1¾"
16-count 1½" x 1½"
18-count 1⅜" x 1⅜"
22-count 1⅛" x 4⅞"

# Baking for Christmas

## DESIGNED BY MIKE VICKERY

Y*our family and friends will be delighted with the treats you whip up! Bake and serve in holiday style with this festive apron and mitt set.*

## Materials

- Eight 10" x 10" pieces of 14-count waste canvas
- Apron
- Oven mitt

## Instructions

1: For Apron, position and baste seven waste canvas pieces to front of apron as shown in photo following manufacturer's instructions. Center and stitch "Ornament" design and "Tree" design as shown, using two strands floss for Cross-Stitch and one strand floss for Backstitch.

2: Remove waste canvas after stitching following manufacturer's instructions.

3: For Oven Mitt, position and baste remaining waste canvas piece to front of oven mitt following manufacturer's instructions. Center and stitch "Ornament" design, using two strands floss for Cross-Stitch and one strand floss for Backstitch.

4: Remove waste canvas after stitching following manufacturer's instructions.

**Ornament**

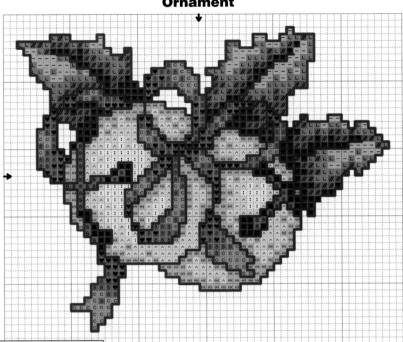

**Ornament
Stitch Count:**
55 wide x 45 high

**Approximate
Design Size:**
11-count 5" x 4⅛"
14-count 4" x 3¼"
16-count 3½" x 2⅞"
18-count 3⅛" x 2½"
22-count 2½" x 2⅛"

| X | B'st | DMC® | ANCHOR® | COLORS |
|---|---|---|---|---|
| ▼ | | 319 | 218 | Very Dk. Pistachio Green |
| // | | 320 | 215 | Med. Pistachio Green |
| δ | | 350 | 11 | Med. Coral |
| C | | 352 | 9 | Lt. Coral |
| L | | 368 | 214 | Lt. Pistachio Green |
| − | | 369 | 1043 | Very Lt. Pistachio Green |
| ■ | | 433 | 358 | Med. Brown |
| s | | 435 | 1046 | Very Lt. Brown |
| ≪ | | 676 | 891 | Lt. Old Gold |
| ∧ | | 677 | 886 | Very Lt. Old Gold |
| : | | 746 | 275 | Off White |
| ♥ | | 817 | 13 | Very Dk. Coral Red |
| ✳ | | 902 | 897 | Very Dk. Garnet |
| Z | | 3046 | 887 | Med. Yellow Beige |
| | ⊟ | 3799 | 236 | Very Dk. Pewter Gray |
| + | | White | 2 | White |

**Tree**

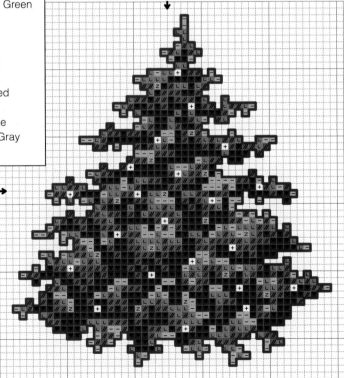

**Tree
Stitch Count:**
47 wide x 52 high

**Approximate
Design Size:**
11-count 4⅜" x 4¾"
14-count 3⅜" x 3¾"
16-count 3" x 3¼"
18-count 2⅝" x 3"
22-count 2⅛" x 2⅜"

# Santa's On His Way

## DESIGNED BY KATHLEEN HURLEY

You'd better watch out! Santa's making his list — but it's impossible to pout while wearing such a cheery outfit.

## Materials

- Two 11" x 13" pieces of 10-count Waste Canvas
  - Sweatshirt
  - Interfacing

## Instructions

1: Position and baste interfacing to wrong side of sweatshirt front and back; next apply waste canvas to front and back of sweatshirt following manufacturer's instructions. Center and stitch "Santa Front" and "Santa Back" designs, using four strands floss for Cross-Stitch and two strands floss for Backstitch.

2: Remove waste canvas after stitching following manufacturer's instructions. Trim interfacing close to stitching.

| X | B'st | DMC® | ANCHOR® | COLORS |
|---|------|------|---------|--------|
| ▌ | | 350 | 11 | Med. Coral |
| ★ | | 413 | 401 | Dk. Pewter Gray |
| ⠂⠂ | | 605 | 50 | Very Lt. Cranberry |
| ⊙ | | 741 | 304 | Med. Tangerine |
| ▣ | | 743 | 302 | Med. Yellow |
| ⓪ | | 762 | 234 | Very Lt. Pearl Gray |
| ◢ | | 813 | 161 | Lt. Blue |
| ▬ | ▭ | 817 | 13 | Very Dk. Coral Red |
| # | | 825 | 162 | Dk. Blue |
| ♥ | | 912 | 209 | Lt. Emerald Green |
| ▽ | ▬ | 939 | 152 | Very Dk. Navy Blue |
| ↑ | | 948 | 1011 | Very Lt. Peach |
| ☐ | | White | 2 | White |

**Santa Front**

**Santa Back**

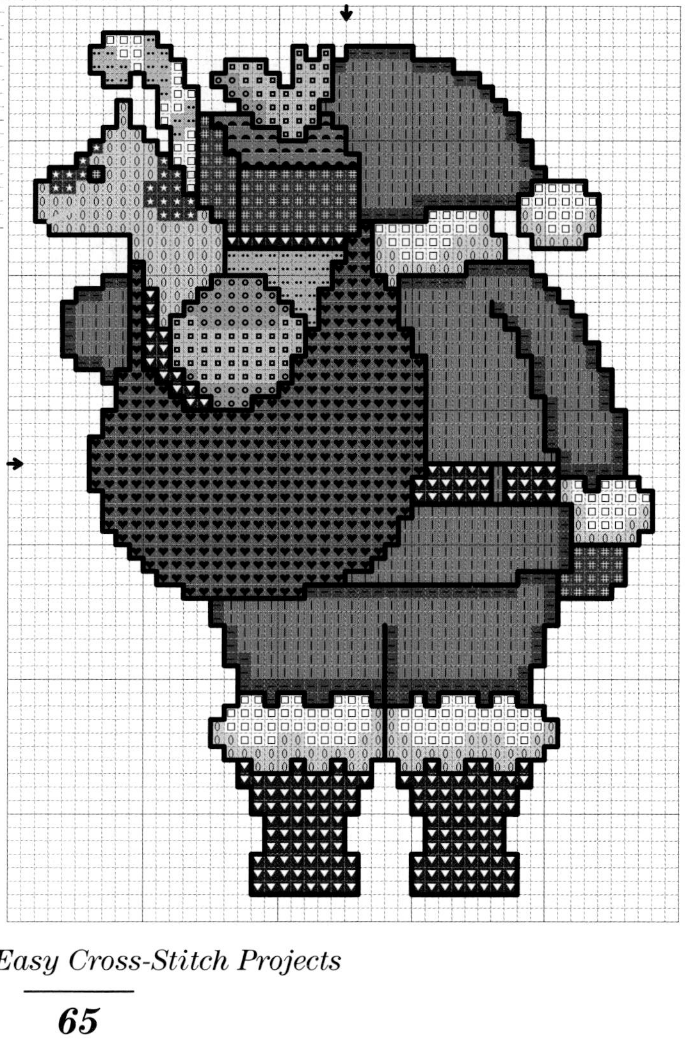

**Santa Front and Back Stitch Count:**
46 wide x 64 high

**Approximate Design Size:**
10-count 4⅝" x 6½"
11-count 4¼" x 5⅞"
14-count 3⅜" x 4⅝"
16-count 2⅞" x 4"
18-count 2⅝" x 3⅝"
22-count 2⅛" x 3"

# Dutch Tulips

## DESIGNED BY MARY B. JONES

*C*ombine a trendy *fashion statement with traditional motifs. These stylized tulips are great stitched on jeans or other fashions using waste canvas.*

## Materials

- Two 3½" x 2¾" pieces and two 6" x 2¾" pieces of 14-count waste canvas
- Capri jeans
- Interfacing

## Instructions

1: For "Yellow" and "Green" designs, position and baste interfacing to wrong side of each front pocket of capri jeans; next apply waste canvas to front of each capri jeans pocket following manufacturer's instructions. Center and stitch each design, using two strands of floss for Cross-Stitch.

2: For "Pink and Blue" and "Purple and Orange" designs, position and baste interfacing to wrong side of each lower leg of capri jeans; next apply waste canvas to front of each capri jeans lower leg following manufacturer's instructions. Center and stitch each design, using two strands of floss for Cross-Stitch.

3: Remove waste canvas after stitching following manufacturer's instructions. Trim interfacing close to stitching.

*101 Quick & Easy Cross-Stitch Projects*

**Green and Yellow
Stitch Count:**
35 wide x 23 high

**Approximate
Design Size:**
11-count 3¼" x 2⅛"
14-count 2½" x 1¾"
16-count 2¼" x 1½"
18-count 2" x 1⅜"
22-count 1⅝" x 1⅛"

| X | DMC® | ANCHOR® | COLORS |
|---|---|---|---|
| ✦ | 553 | 98 | Violet |
| $ | 603 | 62 | Cranberry |
| 7 | 703 | 238 | Chartreuse |
| ✕ | 971 | 316 | Pumpkin |
| ✳ | 973 | 297 | Bright Canary |
| # | 996 | 433 | Med. Electric Blue |

**Pink and Blue and
Purple and Orange
Stitch Count:**
70 wide x 23 high

**Approximate
Design Size:**
11-count 6⅜" x 2⅛"
14-count 5" x 1¾"
16-count 4⅜" x 1½"
18-count 4" x 1⅜"
22-count 3¼" x 1⅛"

**Pink and Purple**

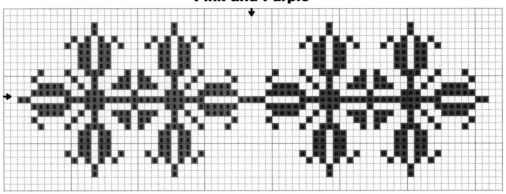

**Purple and Orange**

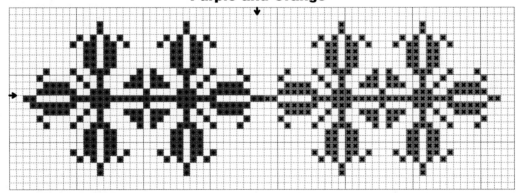

**Green**

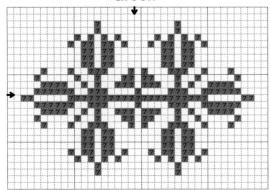

**Yellow**

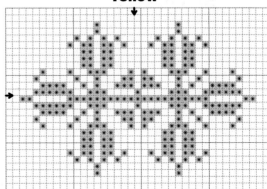

# *Pretty Baby*

## DESIGNED BY URSULA MICHAEL

*Adorable designs stitched on special gifts for wee ones will be the highlight of your next baby shower. You can add these designs to bibs, sleepers, blankets and other items for baby.*

## Materials

- 8" x 8" piece of 14-count Waste Canvas
- 5½" x 7" white 14-count Aida baby bib
- Interfacing
- Sleeper

## Instructions

1: For Sleeper, position and baste interfacing to wrong side of sleeper front and back; next apply waste canvas to front and back of sleeper following manufacturer's instructions. Center and stitch "Baby's Sleeping" design, using two strands floss for Cross-Stitch and one strand floss for Backstitch.

2: Remove waste canvas after stitching following manufacturer's instructions. Trim interfacing close to stitching.

3. For Bib, center and stitch "Baby's Food" design, using two strands floss for Cross-Stitch and one strand floss for Backstitch and French Knot.

| X | B'st | DMC® | ANCHOR® | COLORS |
|---|---|---|---|---|
| + | | 312 | 979 | Very Dk. Baby Blue |
| | | 355 | 1014 | Dk. Terra Cotta |
| ↑ | | 775 | 128 | Very Lt. Baby Blue |
| | | 838 | 380 | Very Dk. Beige Brown |
| × | | 840 | 379 | Med. Beige Brown |
| △ | | 841 | 378 | Lt. Beige Brown |
| * | | 842 | 368 | Very Lt. Beige Brown |
| ○ | | 3325 | 129 | Lt. Baby Blue |
| # | | 3778 | 1013 | Lt. Terra Cotta |
| ‹ | | White | 2 | White |

**Baby's Sleeping**

**Baby's Sleeping Stitch Count:** 26 wide x 24 high

**Approximate Design Size:**
11-count 2⅜" x 2¼"
14-count 1⅞" x 1¾"
16-count 1⅝" x 1½"
18-count 1½" x 1⅜"
22-count 1¼" x 1⅛"

*101 Quick & Easy Cross-Stitch Projects*

**Baby's Food
Stitch Count:**
21 wide x 28 high

**Approximate
Design Size:**
11-count 2" x 2⅝"
14-count 1½" x 2"
16-count 1⅜" x 1¾"
18-count 1¼" x 1⅝"
22-count 1" x 1⅜"

**Baby's Food**

**Baby's Sleeping**

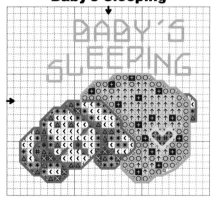

**Babys Food**

| X | B'st | Fr | DMC® | ANCHOR® | COLORS |
|---|------|----|------|---------|--------|
| ◇◇ | ▭ | | 356 | 5975 | Med. Terra Cotta |
| % | ▭ | ● | 400 | 351 | Dk. Mahogany |
| $ | | | 435 | 1046 | Very Lt. Brown |
| # | | | 727 | 293 | Very Lt. Topaz |
| ·· | | | 762 | 234 | Very Lt. Pearl Gray |
| ♦♦ | | | 970 | 316 | Lt. Pumpkin |
| 0 | | | 989 | 242 | Forest Green |
| ( | | | White | 2 | White |

# Sew Much Love

## DESIGNED BY JENNIFER AIKMAN-SMITH

**B**rimming with a palette of colors and bright motifs, this tote is the perfect accessory to carry all of your stitching supplies when you're on the go.

## Materials

• 10" x 14" piece of white 11-count Aida
• 1 yd. trim
• 1 yd. rickrack
• 13" x 15" x 4" canvas zip top tote

## Instructions

1: Center and stitch design onto Aida, using four strands floss for Cross-Stitch and two strands floss for Backstitch and Straight Stitch.
Notes: Trim design to 6⅜" x 10¼".
2: Press under ½" hem on edges of design. Sew trim then rickrack to outside edges of design. Position and sew design to front of tote as shown in photo.

**Stitch Count:**
46 wide x 89 high

**Approximate Design Size:**
11-count 4¼" x 8⅛"
14-count 3⅜" x 6⅜"
16-count 2⅞" x 5⅝"
18-count 2⅝" x 5"
22-count 2⅛" x 4⅛"

| X | B'st Str | | DMC® | ANCHOR® | COLORS |
|---|---|---|---|---|---|
| − | | | 310 | 403 | Black |
| ★ | | | 326 | 59 | Very Dk. Rose |
| ❯ | | | 367 | 217 | Dk. Pistachio Green |
| $ | | | 368 | 214 | Lt. Pistachio Green |
| ) | | | 435 | 1046 | Very Lt. Brown |
| △ | | | 647 | 1040 | Med. Beaver Gray |
| ✳ | | | 648 | 900 | Lt. Beaver Gray |
| •• | | | 743 | 302 | Med. Yellow |
| ↑ | | | 745 | 300 | Lt. Pale Yellow |
| ◻ | | | 796 | 133 | Dk. Royal Blue |
| # | | | 799 | 136 | Med. Delft Blue |
| + | | | 800 | 144 | Pale Delft Blue |
| ○ | | | 3371 | 382 | Black Brown |

# Autumn Mallards

## DESIGNED BY JENNIFER AIKMAN-SMITH

*Add the grandeur of colorful waterfowl to a sweater for your favorite guy. A hand-stitched wearable is like a hug he'll take with him every time he wears it.*

Center and stitch design, using four strands floss for Cross-Stitch and two strands floss for Backstitch.

2: Remove waste canvas after stitching following manufacturer's instructions. Trim interfacing close to stitching.

## Materials

- 10" x 17" piece of 10-count Waste Canvas
- Sweater
- Interfacing

## Instructions

1: Position and baste interfacing to wrong side of sweater; next apply waste canvas to front of sweater following manufacturer's instructions.

**Stitch Count:**
108 wide x 42 high

**Approximate Design Size:**
10-count 10⅞" x 4¼"
11-count 9⅞" x 3⅞"
14-count 7¾" x 3"
16-count 6¾" x 2⅝"
18-count 6" x 2⅜"
22-count 5" x 2"

| X | B'st | DMC® | ANCHOR® | COLORS |
|---|---|---|---|---|
| | | 221 | 897 | Very Dk. Shell Pink |
| | | 310 | 403 | Black |
| | | 367 | 217 | Dk. Pistachio Green |
| | | 368 | 214 | Lt. Pistachio Green |
| | | 434 | 310 | Lt. Brown |
| | | 647 | 1040 | Med. Beaver Gray |
| | | 648 | 900 | Lt. Beaver Gray |
| | | 676 | 891 | Lt. Old Gold |
| | | 680 | 901 | Dk. Old Gold |
| | | 930 | 1035 | Dk. Antique Blue |
| | | 3371 | 382 | Black Brown |
| | | 3752 | 1032 | Very Lt. Antique Blue |
| | | White | 2 | White |

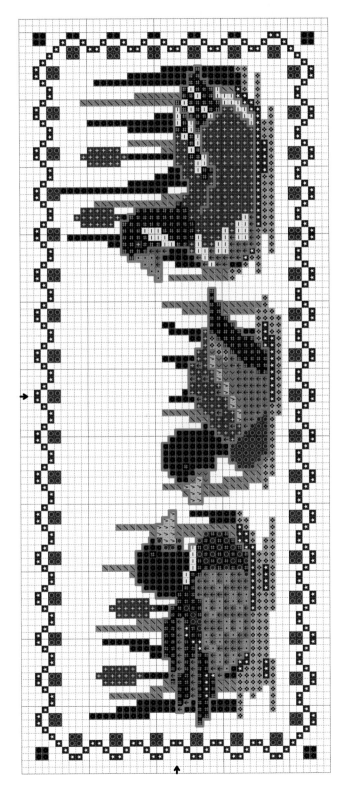

# *Snow Bunnies*

## DESIGNED BY TOM AND FELICIA WILLIAMS

*C*apture the playful spirit of funny bunnies in the snow for the little miss on your gift list.

## *Materials*

- 13" x 70" piece of ash rose 18-count Davosa

## *Instructions*

1: Center and stitch "Pink Snow Bunny" design onto left end and "Blue Snow Bunny" design onto right end of Davosa positioning 5" from short edges as shown in photo, stitching over two threads and using four strands floss for Cross-Stitch and two strands floss for Backstitch.

2: Stay stitch 4" from each short edge; fray edges. Sew ½" hem on each long edge.

**Blue Snow Bunny**

**Blue Snow Bunny Stitch Count:**
83 wide x 110 high

**Approximate Design Size:**
11-count 7⅝" x 10"
14-count 6" x 7⅞"
16-count 5¼" x 6⅞"
18-count 4⅝" x 6⅛"
22-count 3⅞" x 5"
18-count over two
   threads 9¼" x 12¼"

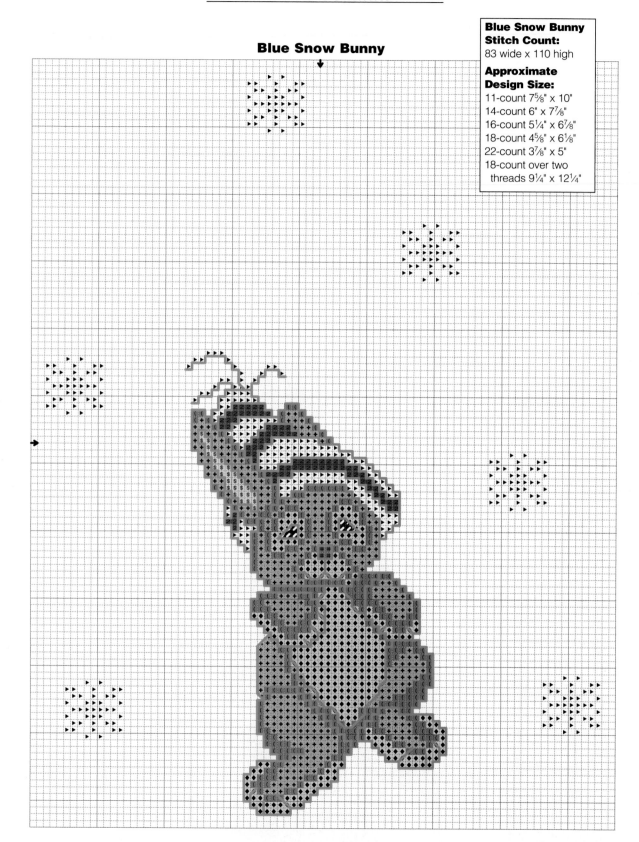

| X | B'st | DMC® | ANCHOR® | COLORS |
|---|------|------|---------|--------|
| ◢ | ▬ | 310 | 403 | Black |
| ( | | 642 | 392 | Dk. Beige Gray |
| + | | 644 | 830 | Med. Beige Gray |
| 2 | | 798 | 131 | Dk. Delft Blue |
| $ | | 818 | 23 | Baby Pink |
| ◆ | | 822 | 390 | Lt. Beige Gray |
| # | | 961 | 76 | Dk. Dusty Rose |
| ▶ | | White | 2 | White |

**Pink Snow Bunny Stitch Count:**
71 wide x 87 high

**Approximate Design Size:**
11-count 6½" x 8"
14-count 5⅛" x 6¼"
16-count 4½" x 5½"
18-count 4" x 4⅞"
22-count 3¼" x 4"
18-count over two
 threads 8" x 9¾"

**Pink Snow Bunny**

*101 Quick & Easy Cross-Stitch Projects*

# Holiday Pals

## DESIGNED BY JACQUELYN FOX

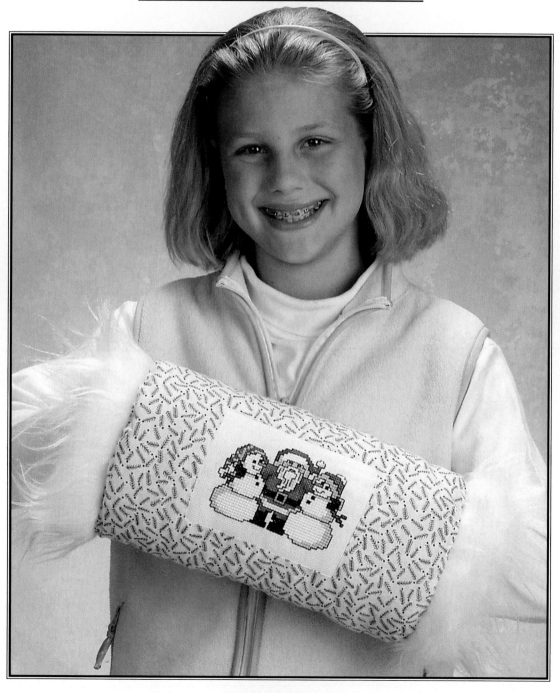

*W*arm your hands and your heart as you stitch this friendly trio. Turn this design into a cozy muff that's perfect for taking the chill off winter days.

## Materials

- 9" x 11" piece of antique white 20-count Lugana®
- ½ yd. fabric
- ½ yd. fleece lining
- Batting
- ½ yd. faux fur

## Instructions

1: Center and stitch design, stitching over two threads and using four strands floss for Cross-Stitch and two strands floss for Backstitch.

Notes: Trim design to 5½" x 6½". From fabric, cut one 12" x 18" piece for front. From fleece lining, cut one 12" x 18" piece for back. From batting, cut one 12" x 18" piece. From faux fur, cut two 3" x 18" pieces. Use ½" seam allowance.

2: Press under ½" hem on design edges. Center and sew design to right side of front as shown in photo.

3: With right sides facing, baste faux fur to long edges of front; next baste batting to wrong side of front. With right sides facing, sew front and back together along long edges; turn right sides out. With right sides facing, sew short edges together, forming muff; turn right sides out.

**Stitch Count:**
48 wide x 32 high

**Approximate Design Size:**
11-count 4⅜" x 3"
14-count 3½" x 2⅜"
16-count 3" x 2"
18-count 2¾" x 1⅞"
22-count 2¼" x 1½"
20-count over two
  threads 4⅞" x 3⅜"

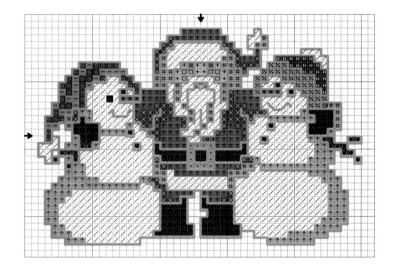

| X | B'st | DMC® | ANCHOR® | COLORS |
|---|---|---|---|---|
| △ | ▭ | 310 | 403 | Black |
| ⑤ | | 312 | 979 | Very Dk. Baby Blue |
| # | | 415 | 398 | Pearl Gray |
| H | | 561 | 212 | Very Dk. Jade |
| % | | 563 | 208 | Lt. Jade |
| T | | 666 | 46 | Bright Red |
| ▢ | | 760 | 1022 | Salmon |
| X | | 816 | 20 | Garnet |
| ○ | | 844 | 1041 | Ultra Dk. Beaver Gray |
| ✳ | | 922 | 1003 | Lt. Copper |
| + | | 950 | 4146 | Lt Desert Sand |
| ↑ | | 3752 | 1032 | Very Lt. Antique Blue |
| ▬ | | 3755 | 140 | Baby Blue |
| · | | 3852 | 307 | Very Dk. Straw |
| ╱ | | White | 2 | White |

# Dapper Duck

## DESIGNED BY BARBARA SESTOK

*Join this darling ducky as he welcomes spring showers! This quick-to-stitch motif worked on waste canvas will add an irresistible highlight to your child's clothing.*

## Materials

- 8" x 10" piece of 14-count Waste Canvas
- Child's denim overalls
- Interfacing

## Instructions

1: Position and baste interfacing to wrong side of overalls; next apply waste canvas to front of overalls following manufacturer's instructions. Center and stitch design, using two strands floss for Cross-Stitch and one strand floss for Backstitch.

2: Remove waste canvas after stitching following manufacturer's instructions. Trim interfacing close to stitching.

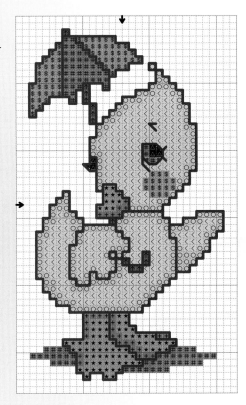

| X | B'st | DMC® | ANCHOR® | COLORS |
|---|------|------|---------|--------|
| < | | 307 | 289 | Lemon |
| △ | ▬ | 310 | 403 | Black |
| $ | | 604 | 55 | Lt. Cranberry |
| + | | 721 | 324 | Med. Orange Spice |
| ★ | | 741 | 304 | Med. Tangerine |
| # | | 809 | 130 | Delft Blue |
| O | | 973 | 297 | Bright Canary |
| ↑ | | 3826 | 349 | Golden Brown |

**Stitch Count:**
29 wide x 52 high

**Approximate Design Size:**
11-count 2⅝" x 4¾"
14-count 2⅛" x 3¾"
16-count 1⅞" x 3¼"
18-count 1⅝" x 3"
22-count 1⅜" x 2⅜"

# My Lady's Roses

## DESIGNED BY MIKE VICKERY

**T**urn a plain white blouse into an elegant array of roses. It's the perfect gift for mom or sister — or yourself!

## Materials

- Blouse with 1½" x 11" white 14-count Aida front placket insert
- One 6" x 6" piece of and two 2" x 4" pieces of 14-count Waste Canvas
- Interfacing

## Instructions

1: Position and baste interfacing to wrong side of left blouse front and each blouse cuff; next apply 6" x 6" piece of waste canvas to left blouse front and each 2" x 4" piece of waste canvas to each blouse cuff following manufacturer's instructions. Center and stitch "Front Placket" design onto insert; "Left Front" and "Cuff" designs onto blouse, using two strands floss for Cross-Stitch and one strand floss for Backstitch.

2: Remove waste canvas after stitching following manufacturer's instructions. Trim interfacing close to stitching.

**Front Placket**

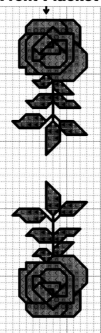

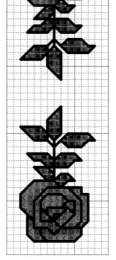

**Left Front**

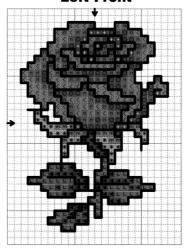

| X | B'st | DMC® | ANCHOR® | COLORS |
|---|------|------|---------|--------|
| O | | 304 | 1006 | Med. Red |
| n | | 666 | 46 | Bright Red |
| ◀ | | 702 | 226 | Kelly Green |
| L | | 704 | 256 | Bright Chartreuse |
| ✳ | | 772 | 259 | Very Lt. Yellow Green |
| + | | 816 | 20 | Garnet |
| m | | 3348 | 264 | Lt. Yellow Green |
| < | | 3705 | 35 | Dk. Melon |
| ▭ | ▬ | 3799 | 236 | Very Dk. Pewter Gray |

**Front Placket Stitch Count:**
11 wide x 94 high

**Approximate Design Size:**
11-count 1" x 8⅝"
14-count ⅞" x 6¾"
16-count ¾" x 5⅞"
18-count ⅝" x 5¼"
22-count ½" x 4⅜"

**Left Front Stitch Count:**
22 wide x 31 high

**Approximate Design Size:**
11-count 2" x 2⅞"
14-count 1⅝" x 2¼"
16-count 1⅜" x 2"
18-count 1¼" x 1¾"
22-count 1" x 1½"

**Cuff**

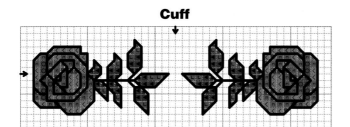

**Cuff Stitch Count:**
42 wide x 11 high

**Approximate Design Size:**
11-count 3⅞" x 1"
14-count 3" x ⅞"
16-count 2⅝" x ¾"
18-count 2⅜" x ⅝"
22-count 2" x ½"

# Eagle Spirit
## DESIGNED BY MIKE VICKERY

Use waste canvas and quick stitches to add the spirit of our national bird to a T-shirt, bag or sweater.

## Materials

- 9" x 15" piece of 10-count waste canvas
- T-shirt
- Interfacing

## Instructions

1: Position and baste interfacing to wrong side of T-shirt; next apply waste canvas to front of T-shirt following manufacturer's instructions. Center and stitch design, using four strands floss for Cross-Stitch and two strands floss for Backstitch.

2: Remove waste canvas after stitching following manufacturer's instructions. Trim interfacing close to stitching.

| X | B'st | DMC® | ANCHOR® | COLORS |
|---|---|---|---|---|
| ✚ | | 310 | 403 | Black |
| ⬤ | | 334 | 977 | Med. Baby Blue |
| ⌗ | | 350 | 11 | Med. Coral |
| ◀ | | 352 | 9 | Lt. Coral |
| ✕ | | 498 | 1005 | Dk. Red |
| 2 | | 502 | 877 | Blue Green |
| ( | | 564 | 206 | Very Lt. Jade |
| ♠ | | 677 | 886 | Very Lt. Old Gold |
| ✳ | | 725 | 305 | Topaz |
| 4 | | 727 | 293 | Very Lt. Topaz |
| ☆ | | 783 | 307 | Med. Topaz |
| ⌶ | | 3325 | 129 | Lt. Baby Blue |
| ✖ | | 3755 | 140 | Baby Blue |
| | ▬ | 3799 | 236 | Very Dk. Pewter Gray |

**Stitch Count:**
88 wide x 28 high

**Approximate Design Size:**
10-count 8⅞" x 2⅞"
11-count 8" x 2⅝"
14-count 6⅜" x 2"
16-count 5½" x 1¾"
18-count 5" x 1⅝"
22-count 4" x 1⅜"

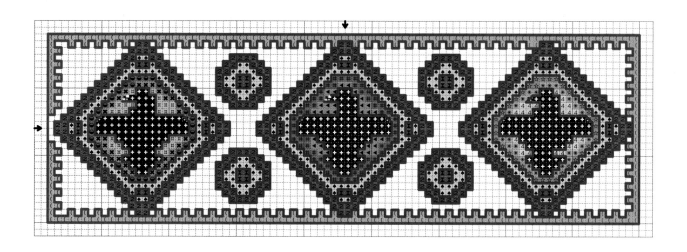

# A Gardener's Delight

## DESIGNED BY MIKE VICKERY

For flowers that last all year long, add these perky floral motifs to a casual denim jumper. They never need watering!

**Blue, Pink, Peach, Lavender and White Stitch Count:**
18 wide x 27 high

**Approximate Design Size:**
10-count 1⅞" x 2¾"
11-count 1⅝" x 2½"
14-count 1⅜" x 2"
16-count 1⅛" x 1¾"
18-count 1" x 1½"
22-count ⅞" x 1¼"

## Materials

- Six 5" x 5" pieces of 10-count waste canvas
- Denim jumper with pockets
- Interfacing

## Instructions

1: Position and baste interfacing to wrong side of jumper; next apply each waste canvas piece to front of jumper above pockets as shown in photo following manufacturer's instructions. Center and stitch one design onto each piece of waste canvas, using four strands floss for Cross-Stitch and two strands floss for Backstitch.

2: Remove waste canvas after stitching following manufacturer's instructions. Trim interfacing close to stitching.

| X | B'st | DMC® | ANCHOR® | COLORS |
|---|------|------|---------|--------|
| ◆◆ | | 210 | 108 | Med. Lavender |
| # | | 605 | 50 | Very Lt. Cranberry |
| ‖ | | 702 | 226 | Kelly Green |
| Y | | 727 | 293 | Very Lt. Topaz |
| $ | | 892 | 33 | Med. Carnation |
| ⊕ | | 976 | 1001 | Med. Golden Brown |
| δ | | 3325 | 129 | Lt. Baby Blue |
| | — | 3799 | 236 | Very Dk. Pewter Gray |
| + | | White | 2 | White |

**Peach** **Blue**

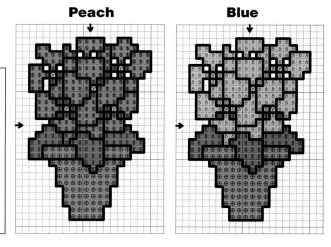

**Lavender**

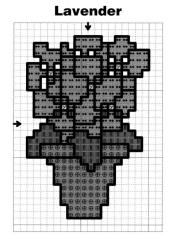

**Pink**

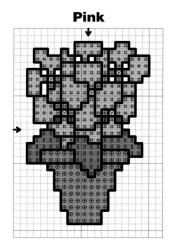

**White**

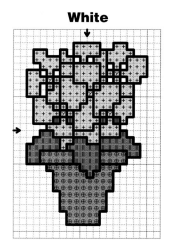

# Star Snowmen

## DESIGNED BY LOIS WINSTON

Proclaim the meaning
of the season with
simple motifs, shading
and basic beading in the
contemporary design.

## Materials

- 4" x 12" piece of 14-count Waste Canvas
- Sweatshirt
- Interfacing

## Instructions

1: Position and baste interfacing to wrong side of sweatshirt; next apply waste canvas to front of sweatshirt following manufacturer's instructions. Center and stitch design, using two strands floss for Cross-Stitch and Backstitch of wording. Use one strand floss for remaining Backstitch. Use one strand coordinating floss for securing beads.

2: Remove waste canvas after stitching following manufacturer's instructions. Trim interfacing close to stitching.

**Stitch Count:**
112 wide x 27 high

**Approximate Design Size:**
11-count 10¼" x 2½"
14-count 8" x 2"
16-count 7" x 1¾"
18-count 6¼" x 1½"
22-count 5⅛" x 1¼"

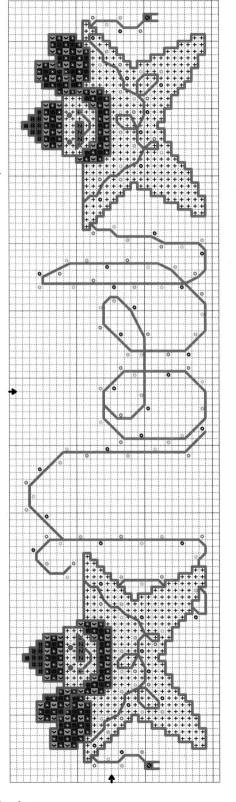

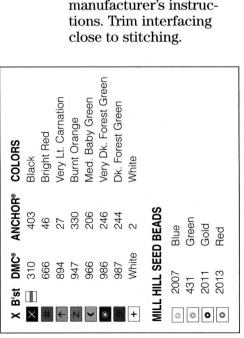

| X | B'st | DMC® | ANCHOR® | COLORS |
|---|---|---|---|---|
| | | 310 | 403 | Black |
| | | 666 | 46 | Bright Red |
| | | 894 | 27 | Very Lt. Carnation |
| | | 947 | 330 | Burnt Orange |
| | | 966 | 206 | Med. Baby Green |
| | | 986 | 246 | Very Dk. Forest Green |
| | | 987 | 244 | Dk. Forest Green |
| | | White | 2 | White |

| MILL HILL SEED BEADS | |
|---|---|
| 2007 | Blue |
| 431 | Green |
| 2011 | Gold |
| 2013 | Red |

# Roses and Violets

## DESIGNED BY ELIZABETH BENTLEY

*O*h so simple,
*yet perfectly elegant.*
*These two floral motifs*
*can be repeated*
*randomly or in rows to*
*create your very own*
*designer creation.*

## Materials

- Ten 4" x 4" pieces of
14-count Waste Canvas
- Knit sweater
- Interfacing

## Instructions

1: Position and baste
interfacing to wrong side
of sweater where motifs
are desired; next apply
waste canvas pieces to
front of sweater follow-
ing manufacturer's
instructions over each
piece of interfacing.
Center and stitch
"Roses" and "Violets"
designs as desired,
using two strands floss
for Cross-Stitch and
one strand floss for
Backstitch.

2: Remove waste canvas
after stitching following
manufacturer's instruc-
tions. Trim interfacing
close to stitching.

**Violets**

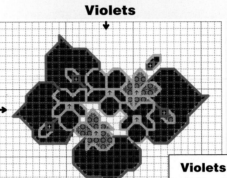

**Roses**

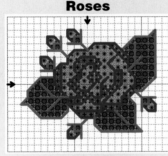

| Violets Stitch Count: | Roses Stitch Count: |
| --- | --- |
| 29 wide x 23 high | 20 wide x 16 high |

| Approximate Design Size: | Approximate Design Size: |
| --- | --- |
| 11-count 2⅝" x 2⅛" | 11-count 1⅞" x 1½" |
| 14-count 2⅛" x 1¾" | 14-count 1½" x 1¼" |
| 16-count 1⅞" x 1½" | 16-count 1¼" x 1" |
| 18-count 1⅝" x 1⅜" | 18-count 1⅛" x 1" |
| 22-count 1⅜" x 1⅛" | 22-count 1 x ¾" |

### Violets

| X | B'st | DMC® | ANCHOR® | COLORS |
| --- | --- | --- | --- | --- |
| ■ | | 208 | 110 | Very Dk. Lavender |
| ◎ | | 210 | 108 | Med. Lavender |
| ↑ | | 444 | 290 | Dk. Lemon |
| | ▬ | 550 | 102 | Very Dk. Violet |
| ✚ | ▬ | 3362 | 263 | Dk. Pine Green |
| ✳ | | 3363 | 262 | Med. Pine Green |

### Roses

| X | B'st | DMC® | ANCHOR® | COLORS |
| --- | --- | --- | --- | --- |
| ✚ | | 223 | 895 | Lt. Shell Pink |
| ✳ | | 224 | 893 | Very Lt. Shell Pink |
| ◎ | | 522 | 860 | Fern Green |
| | ▬ | 3362 | 263 | Dk. Pine Green |
| | ▬ | 3721 | 896 | Dk. Shell Pink |

*101 Quick & Easy Cross-Stitch Projects*

*101 Quick & Easy Cross-Stitch Projects*

# Chapter Three

# Happy Holidays

*Share your stitching talents by making these quick-and-easy projects for holidays throughout the year. Whether you stitch for the pure enjoyment or for creating gifts for friends and family members, you'll love these warm, personal expressions that will be treasured for a lifetime of holidays. These spectacular designs will make decorating your home so much fun for each and every holiday.*

# *Merry Christmas Tray*

## DESIGNED BY JACQUELYN FOX

*H*onor the season by stitching this holiday message. You'll love serving treats to your guests with this festive tray.

## *Materials*

• 13" x 15" piece of white 14-count Aida
• Wooden tray with 9" x 12" design opening

## *Instructions*

1: Center and stitch design, using two strands floss for Cross-Stitch and one strand floss for Backstitch.
2: Position and secure design in tray following manufacturer's instructions.

| X | B'st | DMC® | ANCHOR® | COLORS |
|---|------|------|---------|--------|
| ▲ |  | 319 | 218 | Very Dk. Pistachio Green |
|  | ▬ | 334 | 977 | Med. Baby Blue |
| 2 |  | 666 | 46 | Bright Red |
| # |  | 729 | 890 | Med. Old Gold |
| 8 |  | 814 | 45 | Dk. Garnet |
| ⁄ |  | 816 | 20 | Garnet |
| ✖ |  | White | 2 | White |

**Stitch Count:**
121 wide x 93 high

**Approximate Design Size:**
11-count 11" x 8½"
14-count 8¾" x 6¾"
16-count 7⅝" x 5⅞"
18-count 6¾" x 5¼"
22-count 5½" x 4¼"

# Poinsettia Stocking

## DESIGNED BY MIKE VICKERY

# Materials

*Grace your home with this elegant poinsettia stocking. It's sure to spread holiday cheer even before it's filled with surprises.*

## Materials

• Prefinished 9" x 13½" gold/cream 20-count Lugana® stocking

## Instructions

Center and stitch design, stitching over two threads and using four strands floss for Cross-Stitch and two strands floss for Backstitch.

**Stitch Count:**
61 wide x 82 high

**Approximate Design Size:**
11-count 5⅝" x 7½"
14-count 4⅜" x 5⅞"
16-count 3⅞" x 5⅛"
18-count 3⅜" x 4⅝"
22-count 2⅞" x 3¾"
20-count over two
  threads 3⅛" x 8¼"

| X | B'st | DMC® | ANCHOR® | COLORS |
|---|---|---|---|---|
| | | 319 | 218 | Very Dk. Pistachio Green |
| | | 320 | 215 | Med. Pistachio Green |
| | | 349 | 13 | Dk. Coral |
| | | 351 | 10 | Coral |
| | | 352 | 9 | Lt. Coral |
| | | 368 | 214 | Lt. Pistachio Green |
| | | 700 | 228 | Bright Green |
| | | 702 | 226 | Kelly Green |
| | | 704 | 256 | Bright Chartreuse |
| | | 890 | 218 | Ultra Dk. Pistachio Green |
| | | 3799 | 236 | Very Dk. Pewter Gray |

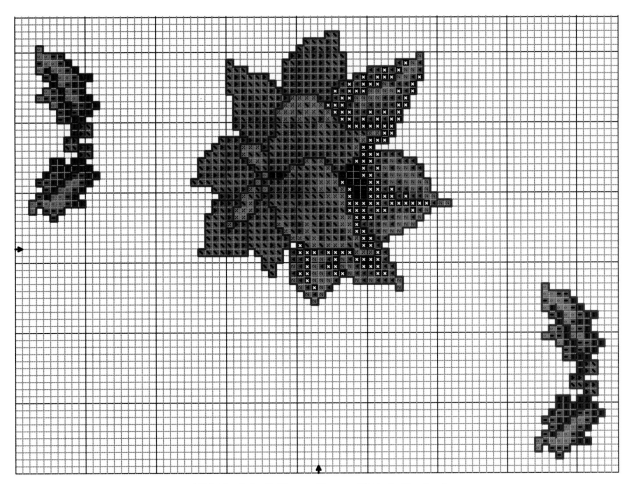

# Oh Christmas Tree

## DESIGNED BY MARY T. COSGROVE

*Surprise your guests with a touch of Christmas cheer in your powder room! Bright Christmas trees and shining stars complement this holiday towel and soap holder.*

## Materials

- 11" x 18" fingertip towel with vanilla 14-count 2½" Aida insert
- 2¾" x 3½" oval Additions™ with vanilla 18-count insert
- 1 yd. ribbon

## Instructions

1: For Towel, center and stitch "Towel" design onto insert, using two strands floss for Cross-Stitch and Backstitch. Use one strand coordinating floss for securing beads.

2: For Soap Holder, center and stitch "Soap Holder" design onto insert, using two strands floss for Cross-Stitch and Backstitch. Thread ribbon through lace edging as shown in photo.

**Soap Holder Stitch Count:**
22 wide x 30 high

**Approximate Design Size:**
11-count 2" x 2¾"
14-count 1⅝" x 2¼"
16-count 1⅜" x 1⅞"
18-count 1¼" x 1¾"
22-count 1" x 1⅜"

**Towel Stitch Count:**
136 wide x 25 high

**Approximate Design Size:**
11-count 12⅜" x 2⅜"
14-count 9¾" x 1⅞"
16-count 8½" x 1⅝"
18-count 7⅝" x 1⅜"
22-count 6¼" x 1⅛"

| X | B'st | DMC® | ANCHOR® | COLORS |
|---|------|------|---------|--------|
| ▬ | | 321 | 9046 | Red |
| ★ | | 3818 | 212 | Ultra Very Dk. Emerald Green |
| 2 | | 3852 | 307 | Very Dk. Straw |
| **MILL HILL SEED BEADS** | | | | |
| ⊙ | | 5106 | | Red Whimsy |

**Soap Holder**

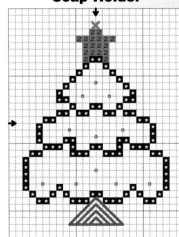

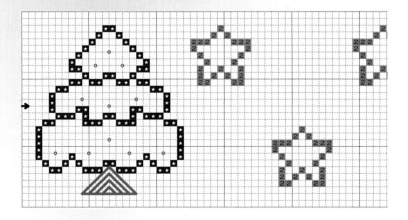

**Towel**

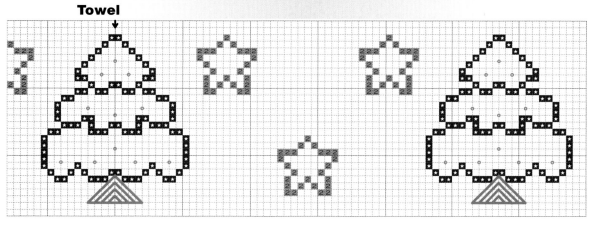

# Reindeer Draft Dodger

## DESIGNED BY DONNA JARVIS

**K**eep your favorite room warm and cozy in more ways than one! Rudolph stitches up quickly on 6-count Aida.

## Materials

- Five 9¾" x 10⅜" pieces of ivory 6-count Aida
- ½ yd. fabric
- Two shank buttons
- Fiberfill
- 2½ yds. trim

## Instructions

1: Center and stitch design onto each piece of Aida, using one strand perle coton for Cross-Stitch and Backstitch.

Notes: Trim each design to 5" x 6". From fabric, cut one 18" x 46" piece. Use ½" seams.

2: Center and sew designs evenly spaced across right side of fabric. Sew trim around edge of each design.

3: For Draft Dodger, with right sides facing, sew long edges of fabric together, forming cylinder. Turn right sides out; finish each end of cylinder. Gather one end of cylinder and sew button over gathers; stuff with fiberfill. Gather remaining end of cylinder and sew button over gathers.

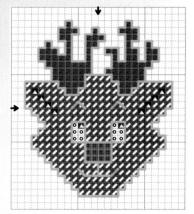

**Stitch Count:**
22 wide x 26 high

**Approximate Design Size:**
6-count 3¾" x 4⅜"
11-count 2" x 2⅜"
14-count 1⅝" x 1⅞"
16-count 1⅜" x 1⅝"
18-count 1¼" x 1½"
22-count 1" x 1¼"

| X | B'st | DMC® (#3 PC) | ANCHOR® | COLORS |
|---|---|---|---|---|
| ◢ | | 433 | 358 | Med. Brown |
| 2 | | 434 | 310 | Lt. Brown |
| # | | 666 | 46 | Bright Red |
| ▲ | ▭ | 938 | 381 | Ultra Dk. Coffee Brown |
| ○ | | White | 2 | White |

# Let It Snow

## DESIGNED BY HOPE MURPHY

**G**littering snowflakes accent this handy huck towel. This design is so quick you'll want to make a few extras for teachers, friends and family members.

## Materials

• 14" x 24½" huck towel with 4½" x 6" white 14-count Aida insert

## Instructions

Center and stitch design, using three strands floss for Cross-Stitch and two strands floss for Backstitch of lettering and snowflakes. Use one strand floss for remaining Backstitch.

| X | B'st | DMC® | ANCHOR® | COLORS |
|---|------|------|---------|--------|
| 2 |  | 775 | 128 | Very Lt. Baby Blue |
|  | — | 797 | 132 | Royal Blue |
| # |  | 3755 | 140 | Baby Blue |
|  | — | 5283 | 702 | Silver Metallic |

**Stitch Count:**
57 wide x 77 high

**Approximate Design Size:**
11-count 5¼" x 7"
14-count 4⅛" x 5½"
16-count 3⅝" x 4⅞"
18-count 3¼" x 4⅜"
22-count 2⅝" x 3½"

# Snowman Ornaments

## DESIGNED BY DARLENE POLACHIC

Trim your tree with these charming snow friends ornaments. These versatile designs can also be mounted on felt for delightful gift package trims.

## Materials for One

- 8" x 10" piece of antique white 14-count Aida
- Scrap of fabric
- Fiberfill
- ¼ yd. ribbon

## Instructions

1: Center and stitch design of choice, using two strands floss for Cross-Stitch and one strand floss for Backstitch.

Notes: Trim design following outline of design for front. From fabric, cut one same as front for back. Use ¼" seam allowance.

2: Baste ribbon ends to top edge of front for hanger. With right sides facing, sew front and back together leaving a small opening for turning. Turn right sides out; fill with fiberfill; slip stitch opening closed.

*101 Quick & Easy Cross-Stitch Projects*

## Wreath

| X | B'st | DMC® | ANCHOR® | COLORS |
|---|------|------|---------|--------|
| ✓ | ▦ | 321 | 9046 | Red |
| ✦✦ | | 437 | 362 | Lt. Tan |
| ◉ | | 445 | 288 | Lt. Lemon |
| $ | ▦ | 701 | 227 | Lt. Green |
| % | | 799 | 136 | Med. Delft Blue |
| ▲ | ▦ | 3371 | 382 | Black Brown |
| 2 | | White | 2 | White |

**Wreath**
**Stitch Count:**
30 wide x 54 high

**Approximate**
**Design Size:**
11-count 2¾" x 5"
14-count 2¼" x 3⅞"
16-count 1⅞" x 3⅜"
18-count 1¾" x 3"
22-count 1⅜" x 2½"

**Candy Cane**
**Stitch Count:**
31 wide x 54 high

**Approximate**
**Design Size:**
11-count 2⅞" x 5"
14-count 2¼" x 3⅞"
16-count 2" x 3⅜"
18-count 1¾" x 3"
22-count 1½" x 2½"

**Birdhouse**
**Stitch Count:**
30 wide x 57 high

**Approximate**
**Design Size:**
11-count 2¾" x 5¼"
14-count 2¼" x 4⅛"
16-count 1⅞" x 3⅝"
18-count 1¾" x 3¼"
22-count 1⅜" x 2⅝"

## Candy Cane

## Birdhouse

# *Symbols of Faith*

## DESIGNED BY MIKE VICKERY

**M**ake the perfect gift set for an avid reader. These inspiring cross motifs stitched on prefinished bookmark and book cover are easy to stitch and need no finishing.

## *Materials*

• Twill book cover that fits a 4" x 7" x 1¼" paper-back book
• 4" x 6" piece of 14-count Waste Canvas
• Prefinished bookmark with 1¾" x 6¾" white 18-count Aida insert

## *Instructions*

1: For Book Cover, apply waste canvas to front of book cover following man-ufacturer's instructions. Center and stitch "Book

**Book Cover**

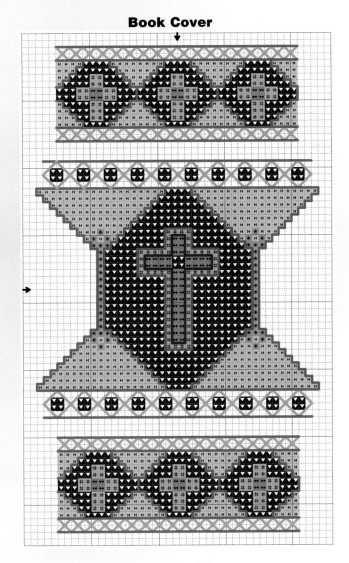

| Book Cover | | | | |
|---|---|---|---|---|
| X | B'st | DMC® | ANCHOR® | COLORS |
| ▼ | ▬ | 336 | 150 | Navy Blue |
| ✳ | | 415 | 398 | Pearl Gray |
| # | | 676 | 891 | Lt. Old Gold |
| H | | 762 | 234 | Very Lt. pearl Gray |
| ◆◆ | ▬ | 3755 | 140 | Baby Blue |
| | ▬ | 3799 | 236 | Very Dk. Pewter Gray |

**Book Cover**

**Stitch Count:**
42 wide x 72 high

**Approximate Design Size:**
11-count 3⅞" x 6⅝"
14-count 3⅞" x 5¼"
16-count 2⅝" x 4½"
18-count 2⅜" x 4"
22-count 2" x 3⅜"

Cover" design, using two stands floss for Cross-Stitch and one strand floss for Backstitch.

2: Remove waste canvas after stitching following manufacturer's instructions.

3: For Bookmark, center and stitch "Bookmark" design onto insert, using two strands floss for Cross-Stitch and one strand floss for Backstitch.

### Bookmark

| X | B'st | DMC® | ANCHOR® | COLORS |
|---|------|------|---------|--------|
| ▲ | | 312 | 979 | Very Dk. Baby Blue |
| ○ | | 341 | 117 | Lt. Blue Violet |
| ♥ | | 498 | 1005 | Dk. Red |
| ^ | | 504 | 1042 | Very Lt. Blue Green |
| ⊕ | | 676 | 891 | Lt. Old Gold |
| | ▬ | 3799 | 236 | Very Dk. Pewter Gray |

**Bookmark**

**Stitch Count:**
24 wide x 105 high

**Approximate Design Size:**
11-count 2¼" x 9⅝"
14-count 1¾" x 7½"
16-count 1½" x 6⅝"
18-count 1⅜" x 5⅞"
22-count 1⅛" x 4⅞"

**Bookmark**

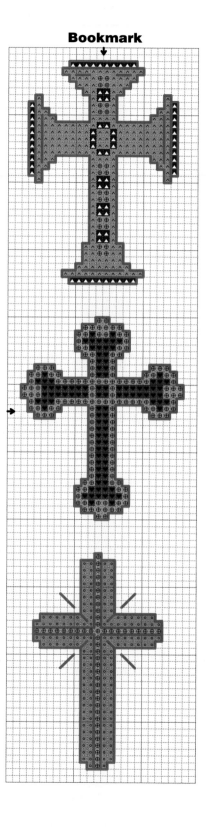

# A Colorful Easter

## DESIGNED BY CHRISTINE A. HENDRICKS

**B**righten your Easter celebration with a sampler full of Easter wonders. Stitch the Peter Rabbit and eggs motifs to hang on your Easter tree. They're sure to bring smiles even faster than chocolate eggs and jelly beans!

## Materials

• One 11" x 13" piece (for A Colorful Easter), seven 8" x 10" pieces (for Ornaments and Tree Topper) of white 14-count Aida
• Scraps of different colored felt
• Seven 6" pieces of ¼" ribbon
• Wooden tree
• Craft glue or glue gun

## Instructions

1: Center and stitch design onto 11" x 13" piece of Aida, using two strands floss for Cross-Stitch, Backstitch and French Knot of lettering. Use one strand floss for remaining Backstitch and French Knot.

2: For Ornaments, center and stitch egg motif from graph onto six 8" x 10" pieces of Aida, using two strands floss for Cross-Stitch and one strand floss for Backstitch.

3: For Tree Topper, center and stitch rabbit motif from graph onto remaining 8" x 10" piece of Aida, using two strands floss for Cross-Stitch and one strand floss for Backstitch.

Note: Following shape of design, trim each egg design and rabbit design one square from stitched design. Trim felt ¼" larger than each design.

3: Glue each trimmed design onto felt. For hangers, glue ends of ribbon to back of each egg design. Glue rabbit design to top of tree. Tie remaining piece of ribbon into a bow and attach to tree as shown in photo or as desired.

| X | B'st | Fr | DMC® | ANCHOR® | COLORS |
|---|------|-----|------|---------|--------|
| + | – | ● | 310 | 403 | Black |
| ✖ | | | 352 | 9 | Lt. Coral |
| ▶ | | | 437 | 362 | Lt. Tan |
| ▼ | | | 602 | 63 | Med. Cranberry |
| ✳ | | | 605 | 50 | Very Lt. Cranberry |
| 7 | | | 727 | 293 | Very Lt. Topaz |
| ( | | | 741 | 304 | Med. Tangerine |
| 2 | | | 794 | 175 | Lt. Cornflower Blue |
| ↑ | | | 927 | 848 | Lt. Gray Green |
| $ | | | 957 | 50 | Pale Geranium |
| L | | | 987 | 244 | Dk. Forest Green |
| ✳ | | | 989 | 242 | Forest Green |
| # | | | 3689 | 49 | Lt. Mauve |
| ◆ | | | 3746 | 1030 | Dk. Blue Violet |
| ☆ | | | White | 2 | White |

**Stitch Count:**
75 wide x 103 high

**Approximate Design Size:**
11-count 6⅞" x 9⅜"
14-count 5⅜" x 7⅜"
16-count 4¾" x 6½"
18-count 4¼" x 5¾"
22-count 3½" x 4¾"

# Witchy Moon

## DESIGNED BY MIKE VICKERY

*T*his frightful friend has no problem working the night shift. Youngsters—and the young at heart—will receive a thrilling welcome on trick or treat night with this bewitching wreath.

# Materials

• 13" x 13" piece of sunflower 22-count Vienna
• Wreath with 8½"-round opening
• Cardboard
• Craft glue or glue gun

# Instructions

1: Center and stitch design, stitching over two threads and using four strands floss for Cross-Stitch and two strands floss for Backstitch.

Note: From cardboard, cut one piece to fit back of wreath.

2: Center and mount design over cardboard. Glue front outside edges of mounted design to back of wreath as shown in photo. Decorate as desired.

**Stitch Count:**
77 wide x 77 high

**Approximate Design Size:**
11-count 7" x 7"
14-count 5½" x 5½"
16-count 4⅞" x 4⅞"
18-count 4⅜" x 4⅜"
22-count 3½" x 3½"
22-count over two
  threads 7" x 7"

| X | B'st | DMC® | ANCHOR® | COLORS |
|---|---|---|---|---|
| ■ | | 413 | 401 | Dk. Pewter Gray |
| V | | 414 | 235 | Dk. Steel Gray |
| ● | | 433 | 358 | Med. Brown |
| > | | 435 | 1046 | Very Lt. Brown |
| * | | 552 | 99 | Med. Violet |
| / | | 554 | 96 | Lt. Violet |
| + | | 945 | 881 | Tawny |
| O | ― | 3799 | 236 | Very Dk. Pewter Gray |

# Bountiful Cornucopia

## DESIGNED BY MIKE VICKERY

You're certain to receive a bountiful harvest of compliments when you stitch this Thanksgiving blessing. Easy-to-stitch harvest images lend a thankful touch to your holiday feast.

## *Materials*

- 11" x 11" piece of cracked wheat 14-count Rustico Aida®
- Mounting board
- Basket
- Craft glue or glue gun

## *Instructions*

1: Center and stitch design, using two strands floss for Cross-Stitch and one strand floss for Backstitch.

Note: From mounting board, cut one piece 5" x 5".

2: Center and mount design over mounting board. Position and glue mounted design to basket as shown in photo.

| X | B'st | DMC® | ANCHOR® | COLORS |
|---|---|---|---|---|
| ‹ | | 349 | 13 | Dk. Coral |
| T | | 351 | 10 | Coral |
| △ | | 435 | 1046 | Very Lt. Brown |
| Z | | 437 | 362 | Lt. Tan |
| ✳ | | 471 | 266 | Very Lt. Avocado Green |
| S | | 472 | 253 | Ultra Lt. Avocado Green |
| + | | 721 | 324 | Med. Orange Spice |
| ○ | | 869 | 944 | Very Dk. Hazelnut Brown |
| ▼ | | 3045 | 888 | Dk. Yellow Beige |
| 3 | | 3046 | 887 | Med. Yellow Beige |
| | ▬ | 3799 | 236 | Very Dk. Pewter Gray |
| › | | 3825 | 323 | Pale Pumpkin |

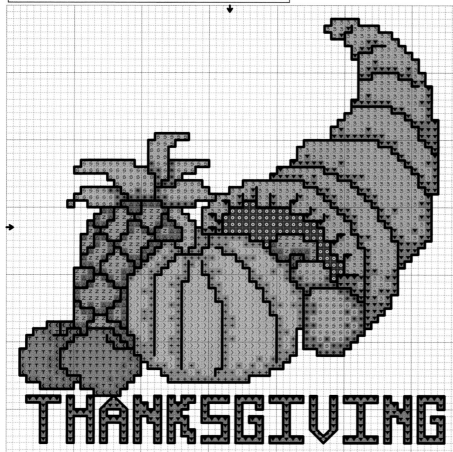

**Stitch Count:**
63 wide x 63 high

**Approximate Design Size:**
11-count 5¾" x 5¾"
14-count 4½" x 4½"
16-count 4" x 4"
18-count 3½" x 3½"
22-count 2⅞" x 2⅞"

# *Baroque Noel*

## DESIGNED BY LOIS WINSTON

*Create a family heirloom to display in your home each Christmas. This stylized framed piece celebrates the joyful carol.*

## *Materials*

- 10" x 20" piece of white 7-count Klostern®

## *Instructions*

Center and stitch design, using six strands floss for Cross-Stitch. Use three strands floss for Backstitch of pine needles and two strands floss for remaining Backstitch.

**Stitch Count:**
94 wide x 25 high

**Approximate Design Size:**
7-count 13½" x 3⅝"
11-count 8⅝" x 2⅜"
14-count 6¾" x 1⅞"
16-count 5⅞" x 1⅝"
18-count 5¼" x 1⅜"
22-count 4⅜" x 1⅛"

| X | B'st | DMC® | ANCHOR® | COLORS |
|---|------|------|---------|--------|
| | ▬ | 310 | 403 | Black |
| ■ | | 321 | 9046 | Red |
| ■ | | 498 | 1005 | Dk. Red |
| ◉ | | 782 | 308 | Dk. Topaz |
| ★ | | 814 | 45 | Dk. Garnet |
| ■ | ▬ | 910 | 229 | Dk. Emerald Green |
| ▨ | | 912 | 209 | Lt. Emerald Green |
| ◆ | | 3818 | 212 | Ultra Very Dk. Emerald Green |

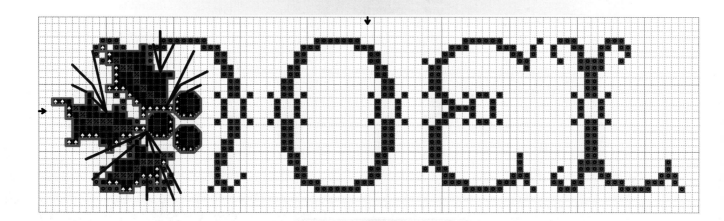

# *Autumn Harvest*

## DESIGNED BY LOIS WINSTON

**B**ring the quiet beauty of Autumn into your dining room with this simple-to-stitch design stitched on a premade bread cloth.

## Materials

• 18" x 18" white 14-count Aida bread cloth

## Instructions

Center and stitch design, positioning on lower left corner 1³⁄₈" from edges, using two strands floss for Cross-Stitch and one strand floss for Backstitch.

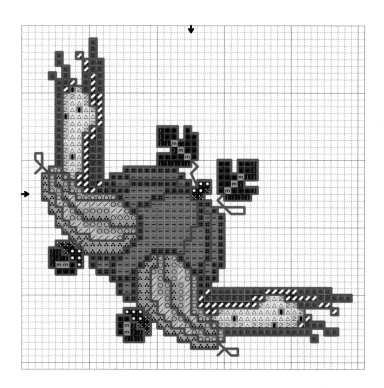

**Stitch Count:**
47 wide x 47 high

**Approximate Design Size:**
11-count 4³⁄₈" x 4³⁄₈"
14-count 3³⁄₈" x 3³⁄₈"
16-count 3" x 3"
18-count 2⁵⁄₈" x 2⁵⁄₈"
22-count 2¹⁄₈" x 2¹⁄₈"

| X | B'st | DMC® | ANCHOR® | COLORS |
|---|------|------|---------|--------|
| ◖ | | 422 | 373 | Lt. Hazelnut Brown |
| ◖ | | 433 | 358 | Med. Brown |
| # | | 720 | 326 | Dk. Orange Spice |
| 2 | | 727 | 293 | Very Lt. Topaz |
| ╱ | | 801 | 359 | Dk. Coffee Brown |
| | ▬ | 938 | 381 | Ultra Dk. Coffee Brown |
| ╱ | | 3011 | 846 | Dk. Khaki Brown |
| ö | | 3012 | 844 | Med. Khaki Brown |
| m | | 3046 | 887 | Med. Yellow Beige |
| ◖ | | 3345 | 268 | Dk. Hunter Green |
| ✱ | | 3346 | 267 | Hunter Green |
| △ | | 3823 | 275 | Ultra Pale Yellow |
| ─ | | 3828 | 888 | Hazelnut Brown |
| ∴ | | 3854 | 1002 | Med. Autumn Gold |
| ╱ | | 3855 | 301 | Lt. Autumn Gold |
| O | | 3856 | 1047 | Ultra Very Lt. Mahogany |

# Land That I Love

## DESIGNED BY CARLA ACOSTA

*C*elebrate the spirit of *C*our great nation all year long with this patriotic pillow.

## *Materials*

• Prefinished pillow sham with 9" x 9" ivory 14-count Aida insert

## *Instructions*

Center and stitch design onto insert, using two strands floss for Cross-Stitch and Backstitch of lettering. Use one strand floss for remaining Backstitch.

**Stitch Count:**
97 wide x 72 high

**Approximate Design Size:**
11-count 8⅞" x 6⅝"
14-count 7" x 5¼"
16-count 6⅛" x 4½"
18-count 5⅜" x 4"
22-count 4½" x 3⅜"

| X | B'st | DMC® | ANCHOR® | COLORS |
|---|------|------|---------|--------|
| T |  | 311 | 148 | Med. Navy Blue |
| + |  | 349 | 13 | Dk. Coral |
| 6 |  | 498 | 1005 | Dk. Red |
| < |  | 712 | 926 | Cream |
| # |  | 725 | 305 | Topaz |
| O |  | 727 | 293 | Very Lt. Topaz |
| * |  | 939 | 152 | Very Dk. Navy Blue |
|  | — | 3371 | 382 | Black Brown |
| △ |  | White | 2 | White |

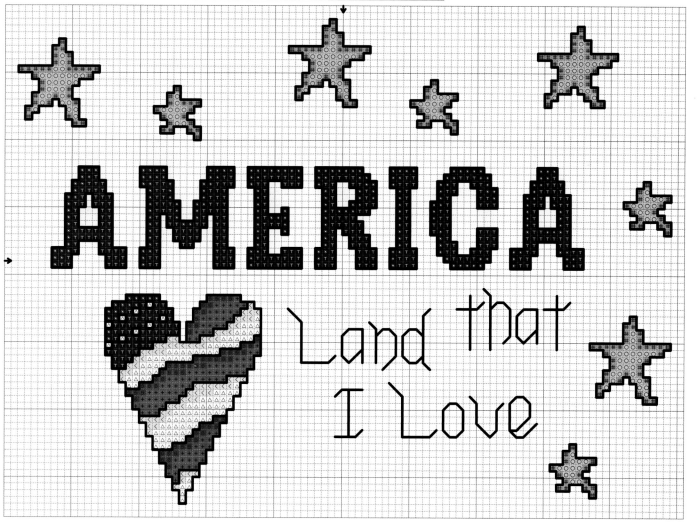

# Easter Flowers

## DESIGNED BY CHRISTINE A. HENDRICKS

A dd a touch of Easter whimsy to your decorating by stitching a decorative band. Wrap around a flowerpot or basket to welcome spring with open arms.

## Materials

- 3⅛" x desired length piece of yellow/white 16-count Stitchband
- Flower pot

## Instructions

Center and stitch design, using two strands floss for Cross-Stitch and one strand floss for Backstitch. Attach to flower pot as shown in photo.

**Stitch Count:**
114 wide x 32 high

**Approximate Design Size:**
11-count 10⅜" x 3"
14-count 8¼" x 2⅜"
16-count 7⅛" x 2"
18-count 6⅜" x 1⅞"
22-count 5¼" x 1½"

| X | B'st | DMC® | ANCHOR® | COLORS |
|---|---|---|---|---|
| | | 310 | 403 | Black |
| | | 553 | 98 | Violet |
| | | 666 | 46 | Bright Red |
| | | 726 | 295 | Lt. Topaz |
| | | 727 | 293 | Very Lt. Topaz |
| | | 906 | 256 | Med. Parrot Green |
| | | 907 | 255 | Lt. Parrot Green |
| | | 961 | 76 | Dk. Dusty Rose |
| | | 970 | 316 | Lt. Pumpkin |
| | | 977 | 1002 | Lt. Golden Brown |
| | | 3716 | 25 | Very Lt. Dusty Rose |
| | | 3747 | 120 | Very Lt. Blue Violet |

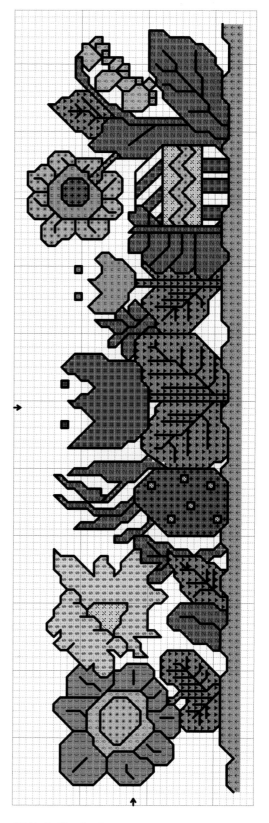

# Treat Toppers

## DESIGNED BY MARY T. COSGROVE

*G*ive a double holiday treat to someone special. Top a jar of goodies with a handmade topper made especially for them.

## Materials for One

• Jar lid cover with 2¾" white 14-count Aida insert

## Instructions

Center and stitch design of choice, using two strands floss for Cross-Stitch, Backstitch, Smyrna Cross and Modified Smyrna Cross.

**For You**

**Holiday Treat**

**For You Stitch Count:**
30 wide x 28 high

**Approximate Design Size:**
11-count 2¾" x 2⅝"
14-count 2¼" x 2"
16-count 1⅞" x 1¾"
18-count 1¾" x 1⅝"
22-count 1⅜" x 1⅜"

**Holiday Treat Stitch Count:**
30 wide x 30 high

**Approximate Design Size:**
11-count 2¾" x 2¾"
14-count 2¼" x 2¼"
16-count 1⅞" x 1⅞"
18-count 1¾" x 1¾"
22-count 1⅜" x 1⅜"

| X | B'st | Smy | Mod | DMC® | ANCHOR® | COLORS |
|---|------|-----|-----|------|---------|--------|
| ◢ | ⊟ | ⊟ | ⊟ | 321 | 9049 | Red |
| ♥ | ⊟ | | | 3818 | 212 | Ultra Very Dk. Emerald Green |

# *Patriotic Checkers*

## DESIGNED BY CARLA ACOSTA

Everyone will want to play along when you stitch this favorite old-fashioned checkers game set.

## *Materials*

• One 11" x 16" piece (for "Game Piece"), one 11" x 10" piece (for "Box") and two 11" x 11" pieces (for "Mug Mats") of beige 14-count Aida
• Wooden tray with 12" x 16" design opening
• Wooden box with 3" x 10¾" design opening

## *Instructions*

1: For Game Board, center and stitch "Game Piece" design onto 11" x 16" piece of Aida, using two strands floss for Cross-Stitch and one strand floss for Backstitch. Position and secure design in opening of tray following manufacturer's instructions.

2: For Box, center and stitch "Box" design onto 11" x 10" piece of Aida, using two strands floss for Cross-Stitch and one strand of floss for Backstitch. Position and secure design in opening of pencil box following manufacturer's instructions.

3: For Mug Mats, center and stitch "Mug Mat 1" and "Mug Mat 2" designs onto 11" x 11" pieces of Aida, using two strands of floss for Cross-Stitch and one strand floss for Backstitch. Trim each design one square from stitched design.

**Box**

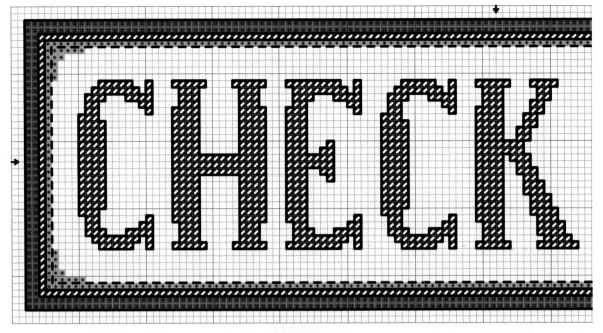

**Mug Mat 1**

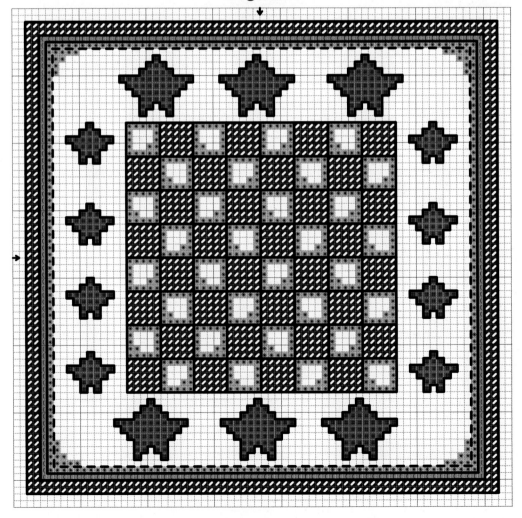

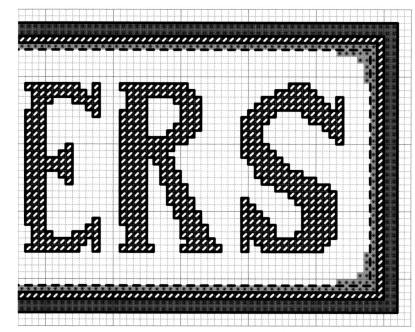

| X | B'st | DMC® | ANCHOR® | COLORS |
|---|---|---|---|---|
| ▦ | | 304 | 1006 | Med. Red |
| ◨ | | 336 | 150 | Navy Blue |
| ✳ | | 738 | 361 | Very Lt. Tan |
| ❨ | | 783 | 307 | Med. Topaz |
| | ▭ | 3371 | 382 | Black Brown |

**Box**
**Stitch Count:**
140 wide x 43 high

**Approximate Design Size:**
11-count 12¾" x 4"
14-count 10" x 3⅛"
16-count 8¾" x 2¾"
18-count 7⅞" x 2⅜"
22-count 6⅜" x 2"

**Mug Mat 1 and Mug Mat 2**
**Stitch Count:**
70 wide x 70 high

**Approximate Design Size:**
11-count 6⅜" x 6⅜"
14-count 5" x 5"
16-count 4⅜" x 4⅜"
18-count 4" x 4"
22-count 3¼" x 3¼"

**Mug Mat 2**

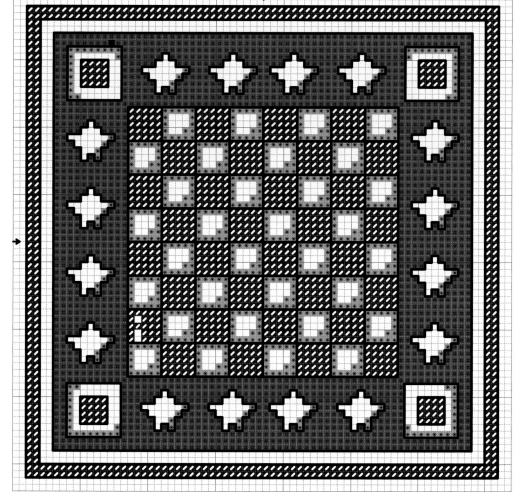

**Game Piece
Stitch Count:**
70 wide x 100 high

**Approximate
Design Size:**
11-count 6⅜" x 9⅛"
14-count 5" x 7¼"
16-count 4⅜" x 6¼"
18-count 4" x 5⅝"
22-count 3¼" x 4⅝"

| X | B'st | DMC® | ANCHOR® | COLORS |
|---|------|------|---------|--------|
| # | | 304 | 1006 | Med. Red |
| ◿ | | 336 | 150 | Navy Blue |
| * | | 738 | 361 | Very Lt. Tan |
| ( | | 783 | 307 | Med. Topaz |
| | ▬ | 3371 | 382 | Black Brown |

**Game Piece**

# Merry Christmas

## DESIGNED BY MARY T. COSGROVE

*C*reate a merry embellishment in a snap for this snap-together mug.

## Materials

- 2½" x 10" piece of white 14-count Stitchband
- Snap-together mug
- FunFoam™
- Craft glue or glue gun

## Instructions

1: Center and stitch design, using two strands floss for Cross-Stitch and Backstitch of bows. Use one strand floss for remaining Backstitch.

Note: From FunFoam, cut one 3½" x 9½" piece for backing.

2: Remove drink insert from mug; place backing, then design around insert as shown in photo, gluing if desired. Replace drink insert into mug.

**Stitch Count:**
47 wide x 18 high

**Approximate Design Size:**
11-count 4⅜" x 1⅝"
14-count 3⅜" x 1⅜"
16-count 3" x 1⅛"
18-count 2⅝" x 1"
22-count 2⅛" x ⅞"

| X | B'st | DMC® | ANCHOR® | COLORS |
|---|------|------|---------|--------|
| | ▭ | 310 | 406 | Black |
| ◨ | | 321 | 9046 | Red |
| ★ | ▭ | 700 | 228 | Bright Green |

# Snowmen at Play

## DESIGNED BY MIKE VICKERY

*S*titch jolly holiday snowmen on this lovely afghan and be ready to snuggle up when the first signs of winter arrive. Each happy snowman can be used alone to decorate coordinating pillows, pictures or other accessories.

## Materials

• 55" x 55" piece of antique white 18-count Tannenbaum
• 6½ yds. of ⅞"-wide double fold bias tape

## Instructions

1: Center and stitch each design twice onto center panels of afghan, stitching over two threads and using six strands floss for Cross-Stitch and two strands floss for Backstitch.
2: Encase outside edges of afghan with bias tape, folding corners as you go.

### Snowman With Umbrella

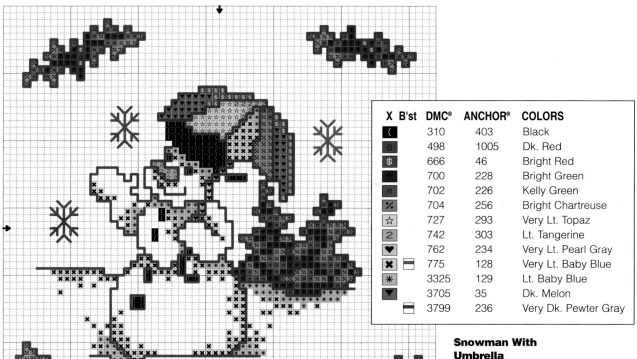

| X | B'st | DMC® | ANCHOR® | COLORS |
|---|------|------|---------|--------|
| ( | | 310 | 403 | Black |
| S | | 498 | 1005 | Dk. Red |
| $ | | 666 | 46 | Bright Red |
| ↑ | | 700 | 228 | Bright Green |
| n | | 702 | 226 | Kelly Green |
| % | | 704 | 256 | Bright Chartreuse |
| ☆ | | 727 | 293 | Very Lt. Topaz |
| 2 | | 742 | 303 | Lt. Tangerine |
| ♥ | | 762 | 234 | Very Lt. Pearl Gray |
| ✖ | ▭ | 775 | 128 | Very Lt. Baby Blue |
| ✳ | | 3325 | 129 | Lt. Baby Blue |
| ▼ | ▭ | 3705 | 35 | Dk. Melon |
| | ▭ | 3799 | 236 | Very Dk. Pewter Gray |

**Snowman With Umbrella Stitch Count:**
60 wide x 63 high

**Approximate Design Size:**
11-count 5½" x 5¾"
14-count 4⅜" x 4½"
16-count 3¾" x 4"
18-count 3⅜" x 3½"
22-count 2¾" x 2⅞"
18-count over two
  threads 6¾" x 7"

| X | B'st | DMC® | ANCHOR® | COLORS |
|---|------|------|---------|--------|
| ( | | 310 | 403 | Black |
| 5 | | 498 | 1005 | Dk. Red |
| $ | | 666 | 46 | Bright Red |
| ↑ | | 700 | 228 | Bright Green |
| n | | 702 | 226 | Kelly Green |
| % | | 704 | 256 | Bright Chartreuse |
| ☆ | | 727 | 293 | Very Lt. Topaz |
| 2 | | 742 | 303 | Lt. Tangerine |
| ♥ | | 762 | 234 | Very Lt. Pearl Gray |
| ✖ | ▭ | 775 | 128 | Very Lt. Baby Blue |
| ✳ | | 3325 | 129 | Lt. Baby Blue |
| ▼ | | 3705 | 35 | Dk. Melon |
| | ▭ | 3799 | 236 | Very Dk. Pewter Gray |

**Snowman With Top Hat Stitch Count:**
66 wide x 60 high

**Approximate Design Size:**
11-count 6" x 5½"
14-count 4¾" x 4⅜"
16-count 4⅛" x 3¾"
18-count 3¾" x 3⅜"
22-count 3" x 2¾"
18-count over two
  threads 7⅜" x 6¾"

## Snowman With Top Hat

# God Bless America

## DESIGNED BY CARLA ACOSTA

*101 Quick & Easy Cross-Stitch Projects*

The bright colors of this quilted banner will proudly display your heartfelt message honoring our great nation.

## Materials

- One 4" x 23¾" piece and two 4" x 13¾" pieces of white 14-count Aida
  - ¼ yd. of fabric No. 1
  - ½ yd. of fabric No. 2
  - Batting
  - Three ⅞" rings

## Instructions

1: Center and stitch three "Heart" designs onto one 4" x 13¾" piece of Aida leaving 24 squares between designs; five "Heart" designs onto 4" x 25¾" piece leaving 30 squares between designs; and "God Bless America" onto remaining 4" x 13¾" piece of Aida, using two strands floss for Cross-Stitch and one strand floss for Backstitch.

Notes: From fabric No. 1, cut two 4" x 13¾" for A pieces and two 4" x 25¾" for B pieces. From fabric No. 2, cut one 13" x 13" for C piece and one 22" x 25¾" for back. From batting, cut one same as back. Use ½" seam allowance.

2: For Wall Hanging, with right sides facing, sew designs, A, B and C pieces together according to Front Assembly Diagram, forming Front. Baste batting to wrong side of front. With right sides facing, sew front and back together leaving a small opening; turn right sides out. Slip stitch opening closed; press.

4: Sew rings to top edge of wall hanging as shown in photo.

**Front Assembly Diagram**

**Heart**

| X | B'st | ANCHOR® | DMC® | COLORS |
|---|------|---------|------|--------|
| ◆◆ | | 133 | 796 | Cobalt Blue Dk. |
| | ▬ | 403 | 310 | Black |
| # | | 9046 | 321 | Christmas Red |
| ✎ | | 2 | White | White |

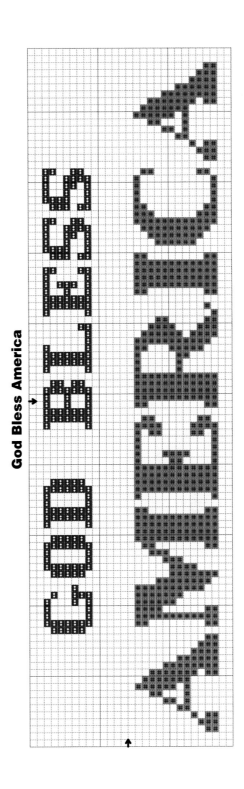

**God Bless America**

**Heart**
**Stitch Count:**
29 wide x 26 high

**Approximate**
**Design Size:**
11-count 2⅝" x 2⅜"
14-count 2⅛" x 1⅞"
16-count 1⅞" x 1⅝"
18-count 1⅝" x 1½"
22-count 1⅜" x 1¼"

**God Bless**
**America**
**Stitch Count:**
95 wide x 25 high

**Approximate**
**Design Size:**
11-count 9⅝" x 2⅜"
14-count 6⅞" x 1⅞"
16-count 6" x 1⅝"
18-count 5⅜" x 1⅜"
22-count 4⅜" x 1⅛"

*Special Days*

*Special Days presents a treasure trove of delightful images to suit all occasions. Welcome a newborn into the world with a special nursery gift. Commemorate a wedding day or a golden anniversary. Make a unique desk set for Dad or stitch a loving verse for Mother. Surprise a special teacher with a quick-to-stitch bookmark. No matter what the occasion is you'll find your labor-of-love gift is one that touches the heart.*

# Sleep Tight

## Designed by Ursula Michael

*Precious little ones will be eager to drift off to dreamland when they snuggle up with this adorable teddy bear.*

## Materials

• 43" x 53" white 4-count fabric baby afghan

## Instructions

Center and stitch design onto afghan, using six strands floss for Cross-Stitch and two strands floss for Backstitch.

**Stitch Count:**
50 wide x 57 high

**Approximate Design Size:**
4-count 12½" x 14¼"
11-count 4⅝" x 5¼"
14-count 3⅛" x 3⅝"
16-count 3⅛" x 3⅝"
18-count 2⅞" x 2⅝"
22-count 2⅜" x 4⅞"

| X | B'st | DMC® | ANCHOR® | COLORS |
|---|---|---|---|---|
| | | 309 | 42 | Dk. Rose |
| | | 435 | 1046 | Very Lt. Brown |
| | | 437 | 362 | Lt. Tan |
| | | 726 | 295 | Lt. Topaz |
| | | 739 | 387 | Ultra Very Lt. Tan |
| | | 747 | 158 | Very Lt. Sky Blue |
| | | 818 | 23 | Baby Pink |
| | | 826 | 161 | Med. Blue |
| | | 827 | 160 | Very Lt. Blue |
| | | 910 | 229 | Dk. Emerald Green |
| | | 913 | 204 | Med. Nile Green |
| | | 955 | 206 | Lt. Nile Green |
| | | 3326 | 36 | Lt. Rose |
| | | 3371 | 382 | Black Brown |
| | | 3779 | 868 | Ultra Very Lt. Terra Cotta |

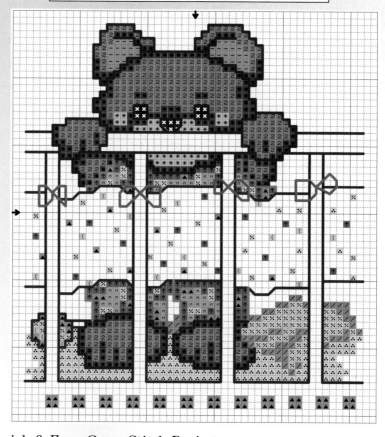

*101 Quick & Easy Cross-Stitch Projects*

**142**

# Seasonal Needlerolls

## DESIGNED BY SUSAN STADLER

*Surprise a dear friend with the gift of an old-fashioned needleroll pincushion. They'll think you spent hours and hours stitching, but this gift is really quick and easy.*

## Materials

• 8" piece of 8"-wide white 28-count Stitchband (for "Summer Afternoons")
• 8" piece of 8"-wide natural 28-count Stitchband (for "Spring Mornings")
• Ladybug charm (for Summer Afternoons)
• Butterfly charm (for Summer Afternoons)
• Two bee charms (for Summer Afternoons)
• Hummingbird charm (for Spring Mornings)
• 8" piece of ½"-wide trim(for Summer Afternoons)
• 8" piece of ½"-wide lace(for Spring Mornings)
• 1⅔ yds. of ⅛" ribbon
• Batting

## Instructions

1: For Summer Afternoons, center and stitch design onto white stitchband, stitching over two threads and using two strands floss for Cross-Stitch and Backstitch and one strand floss for Rhodes Stitch. For Spring Mornings, center and stitch design onto natural Stitchband, stitching over two threads using two strands floss for Cross-Stitch, Backstitch, French Knot, Smyrna Cross and Spider Web Rose. Use one strand floss for Rhodes Stitch.

2: Sew lace or trim to top edge of each Stitchband ½" above stitching. Sew charms in place as shown in photo.

3: For each Needleroll, beginning ten threads in from innermost edges of top and bottom Stitchband borders, remove the next four threads. With matching floss, Hemstitch outer edges of drawn thread areas to form channels for ribbon drawstrings. With right sides together and aligning drawstring channels and edges of trim, sew side edges together with ½" seam allowance; trim seams and turn right sides out.

4: For drawstrings, cut ribbon into four equal pieces and weave in channels. Stuff with batting and tie drawstrings into bows.

**Summer Afternoons**

## Spring Mornings

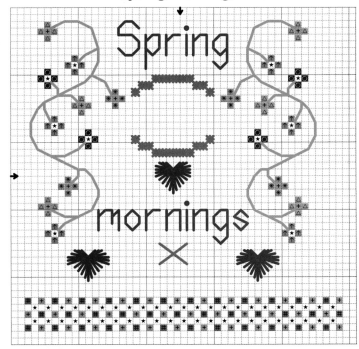

**Spring Mornings Stitch Count:**
47 wide x 46 high

**Approximate Design Size:**
11-count 4⅜" x 4¼"
14-count 3⅜" x 3⅜"
16-count 3" x 2⅞"
18-count 2⅝" x 2⅝"
22-count 2⅛" x 2⅛"
28-count over two
   threads 3⅜" x 3⅜"

### Spring Mornings

| X | B'st | Fr | RhH | Smy | SpW | KREINIK SILK MORI® | DMC® | COLORS |
|---|---|---|---|---|---|---|---|---|
| ◯ | | | ▱ | | | 1094 | 3727 | Medium Wood Violet |
| ⌗ | | | | | | 4204 | 524 | Medium Sage |
| + | | ▱ | | | | 4206 | 522 | Dark Sage |
| △ | | | | | | 5093 | 3755 | Light Royal Blue |
| ✳ | | | | | | 6076 | 554 | Dark Mauve Mist |
| ↑ | ▱ | ● | | | | 6127 | 327 | Very Dark Dusty Lavender |
| ★ | | | | ▱ | | 8000 | 3865 | Soft White |
| | | | | | ▱ | 6127 | 327 | Very Dark Dusty Lavender (one strand) held with |
| | | | | | | 8000 | 3865 | Soft White (one strand) |

### Summer Afternoons

| X | B'st | RhV | KREINIK SILK MORI® | DMC® | COLORS |
|---|---|---|---|---|---|
| ✳ | | | 1116 | 304 | Dark Christmas Red |
| ◯ | | | 1119 | 814 | Garnet |
| | ▱ | ▱ | 2014 | 3821 | Medium Gold |
| ↑ | ▱ | | 4164 | 502 | Med. Victorian Green |
| + | ▱ | | 5013 | 797 | Light Navy |
| △ | ▱ | | 5073 | 800 | Light Country Blue |
| | ▱ | | 7134 | 831 | Medium Bark |

**Stitch Count:**
47 wide x 44 high

**Approximate Design Size:**
11-count 4⅜" x 4"
14-count 3⅜" x 3¼"
16-count 3" x 2¾"
18-count 2⅝" x 2½"
22-count 2⅛" x 2"
28-count over two
   threads 3⅜" x 3¼"

# Wild Ducks

## DESIGNED BY MIKE VICKERY

*D*ucks are a favorite masculine decorating theme. This handsome desk set would look great in any man's office or study and is an ideal Father's Day gift.

## Materials

• One 9" x 13" piece, one 8" x 10" piece and one 8" x 8" piece of oatmeal 14-count Fiddler's Cloth
• Wooden box with 3" x 7¼" design opening
• Glass oval paperweight with 2½" x 4" design opening
• Acrylic caddy with 4" x 10½" design opening

## Instructions

1: For Wooden Box, center and stitch "Box" design onto 9" x 13" piece of Fiddler's Cloth, using two strands floss for Cross-Stitch and one strand floss for Backstitch. Position and secure design in box following manufacturer's instructions.

2: For Paperweight, center and stitch "Paperweight" design onto 8" x 10" piece of Fiddler's Cloth, using two strands floss for Cross-Stitch and one strand floss for Backstitch. Position and secure design in paperweight following manufacturer's instructions.

3: For Caddy, center and stitch "Caddy" design onto 8" x 8" piece of Fiddler's Cloth, using two strands floss for Cross-Stitch and one strand floss for Backstitch. Position and secure design in caddy following manufacturer's instructions.

# Wild Ducks

### Box

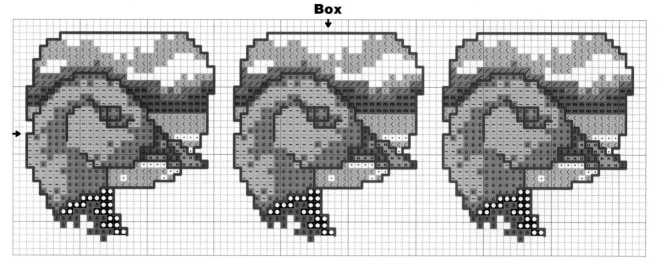

**Box**
**Stitch Count:**
90 wide x 31 high

**Approximate
Design Size:**
11-count 8¼" x 2⅞"
14-count 6½" x 2¼"
16-count 5⅝" x 2"
18-count 5" x 1¾"
22-count 4⅛" x 1½"

### Paperweight

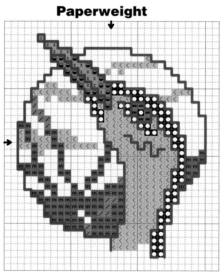

### Caddy

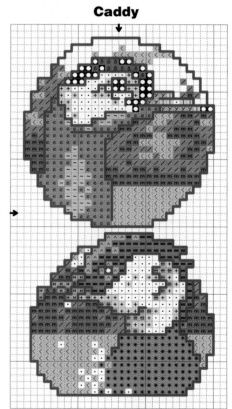

| X | B'st | Fr | DMC® | ANCHOR® | COLORS |
|---|---|---|---|---|---|
| ◙ | | ◉ | 310 | 403 | Black |
| m | | | 320 | 215 | Med. Pistachio Green |
| / | | | 368 | 214 | Lt. Pistachio Green |
| ß | | | 414 | 235 | Dk. Steel Gray |
| H | | | 415 | 398 | Pearl Gray |
| = | | | 435 | 1046 | Very Lt. Brown |
| ^ | | | 437 | 362 | Lt. Tan |
| ⧣ | | | 644 | 830 | Med. Beige Gray |
| ◖ | | | 720 | 326 | Dk. Orange Spice |
| ⲓ | | | 722 | 323 | Lt. Orange Spice |
| y | | | 725 | 305 | Topaz |
| ı | | | 727 | 293 | Very Lt. Topaz |
| + | | | 822 | 390 | Lt. Beige Gray |
| ✳ | | | 3032 | 903 | Med. Mocha Brown |
| < | | | 3325 | 129 | Lt. Baby Blue |
| e | | | 3778 | 1013 | Lt. Terra Cotta |
| ~ | | | 3779 | 868 | Ultra Very Lt. Terra Cotta |
| | ▬ | | 3799 | 236 | Very Dk. Pewter Gray |
| • | | | White | 2 | White |

**Paperweight**
**Stitch Count:**
28 wide x 33 high

**Approximate
Design Size:**
11-count 2⅝" x 3"
14-count 2" x 2⅜"
16-count 1¾" x 2⅛"
18-count 1⅝" x 1⅞"
22-count 1⅜" x 1½"

**Caddy**
**Stitch Count:**
28 wide x 53 high

**Approximate
Design Size:**
11-count 2⅝" x 4⅞"
14-count 2" x 3⅞"
16-count 1¾" x 3⅜"
18-count 1⅝" x 3"
22-count 1⅜" x 2½"

# Balloons

## DESIGNED BY PATRICIA MALONEY MARTIN

**P**ersonalize any birthday gift with this quick-to-stitch balloon motif. The recipient will love the card as much as the gift.

## Materials

• 6" x 6" piece of ecru 14-count perforated paper
• Greeting card with 2½" x 4" design opening

## Instructions

Center and stitch design, using two strands floss for Cross-Stitch and Backstitch of balloon strings. Use one strand floss for remaining Backstitch. Trim design and insert into card following manufacturer's instructions.

**Stitch Count:**
22 wide x 32 high

**Approximate Design Size:**
11-count 2" x 3"
14-count 1⅝" x 2⅜"
16-count 1⅜" x 2"
18-count 1¼" x 1¾"
22-count 1" x 1½"

| X | B'st | DMC® | ANCHOR® | COLORS |
|---|---|---|---|---|
| ( | | 208 | 110 | Very Dk. Lavender |
| ▶ | | 210 | 108 | Med. Lavender |
| | ▬ | 310 | 403 | Black |
| 2 | | 444 | 290 | Dk. Lemon |
| ✚ | | 445 | 288 | Lt. Lemon |
| ◆ | | 794 | 175 | Lt. Cornflower Blue |
| ◢ | | 798 | 131 | Dk. Delft Blue |
| $ | | 3687 | 68 | Mauve |
| # | | 3689 | 49 | Lt. Mauve |
| ✖ | | White | 2 | White |

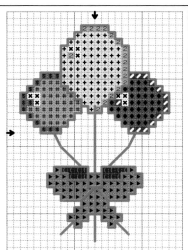

*101 Quick & Easy Cross-Stitch Projects*

# *Delilah*

## DESIGNED BY CAROLYN MANNING

Bunny rabbits are so loveable and you're sure to fall in love with Delilah as she tiptoes through the flowers.

## *Materials*

• 45" x 45" piece of 7-count white Country Aida
• 1 yd. ⅝" ribbon

## *Instructions*

1: Stitch "Delilah's Flowers" design in lower right corner beginning 6" from edges, using six strands floss for Cross-Stitch and two strands floss for Backstitch. Stitch

"Delilah" design on each side of "Delilah's Flowers" leaving 8" between designs as shown in photo and using six strands floss for Cross-Stitch and two strands floss for Backstitch.

2: Stay stitch 4" from outside edges; fray edges, forming afghan.

Note: Cut ribbon in half.

3: Tie each ribbon piece into a bow and attach to afghan as shown.

**Delilah**

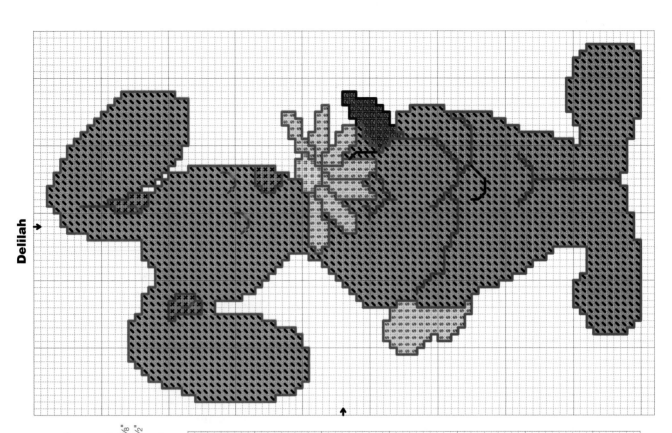

**Delilah**
**Stitch Count:**
53 wide x 88 high

**Approximate**
**Design Size:**
11-count 4⅞" x 8"
14-count 3⅞" x 6⅜"
16-count 3⅜" x 5½"
18-count 3" x 5"
22-count 2½" x 4"

**Delilah's Flowers**
**Stitch Count:**
64 wide x 63 high

**Approximate**
**Design Size:**
11-count 5⅞" x 5¾"
14-count 4⅝" x 4½"
16-count 4" x 4"
18-count 3⅝" x 3½"
22-count 3" x 2⅞"

| X | B'st | DMC® | ANCHOR® | COLORS |
|---|---|---|---|---|
| ▯ | | 839 | 360 | Dk. Beige Brown |
| | | 3078 | 292 | Very Lt. Golden Yellow |
| ▯ | | 3354 | 74 | Lt. Dusty Rose |
| # | | 3363 | 262 | Med. Pine Green |
| ✖ | | 3782 | 899 | Lt. Mocha Brown |
| ▨ | | Ecru | 387 | Ecru |
| ◨ | | | | |
| ⑨ | | | | |

**Delilah's Flowers**

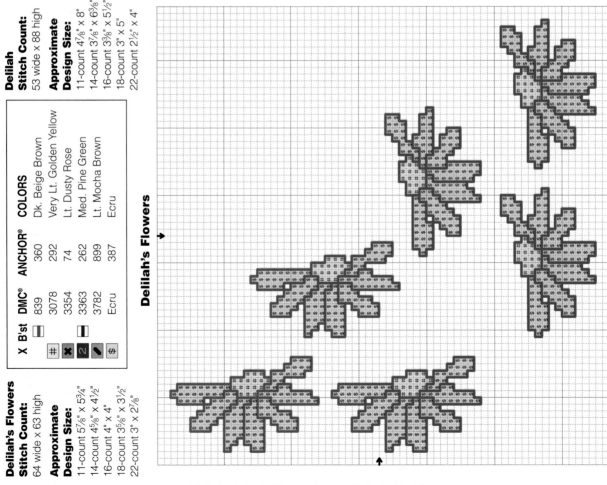

*101 Quick & Easy Cross Stitch Projects*

# Blocks

## DESIGNED BY PATRICIA MALONEY MARTIN

*Building blocks are not only fun to play with, they're also fun to stitch! Add this quick-and-easy design to any lamp shade for the perfect child's room accessory.*

## Materials

- 9" x 20 piece of white 20-count Aida
- Lamp shade
- Lamp base
- 1 yd. baby rickrack
- ¾ yd. gathered lace

## Instructions

1: Center and stitch design, stitching over two threads and using four strands floss for Cross-Stitch and two strands floss for Backstitch.

2: Position and secure design onto lamp shade following manufacturer's instructions. Embellish lamp shade as shown in photo or as desired.

**Stitch Count:**
28 wide x 28 high

**Approximate Design Size:**
11-count 2⅝" x 2⅝"
14-count 2" x 2"
16-count 1¾" x 1¾"
18-count 1⅝" x 1⅝"
22-count 1⅜" x 1⅜"
20-count over two threads 2⅞" x 2⅝"

| X | B'st | DMC® | ANCHOR® | COLORS |
|---|---|---|---|---|
| | | 208 | 110 | Very Dk. Lavender |
| | | 210 | 108 | Med. Lavender |
| | | 310 | 403 | Black |
| | | 444 | 290 | Dk. Lemon |
| | | 564 | 206 | Very Lt. Jade |
| | | 794 | 175 | Lt. Cornflower Blue |
| | | 798 | 131 | Dk. Delft Blue |
| | | 3685 | 1028 | Very Dk. Mauve |
| | | 3689 | 49 | Lt. Mauve |

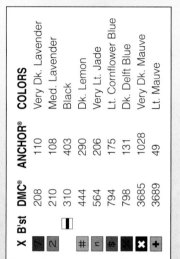

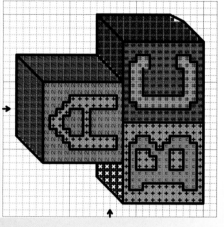

# Everything's Ducky

## DESIGNED BY PATRICIA MALONEY MARTIN

**B**abies are the most precious gift in the world! Stitch this adorable set including shoes, visor, shirt and bottlecover for the new arrival in your life.

## Materials

• Pair of white baby shoes with 14-count Aida design area
• Baby visor with white 14-count Aida design area
• Baby T-shirt with 2½" x 9¾" white 14-count Aida insert
• Baby bottle cover with white 14-count Sal-Em™ cloth panel

## Instructions

1: For Shoes, center and stitch "Shoe" design onto each baby shoe, using two strands floss for Cross-Stitch and one strand floss for Backstitch.
2: For Visor, center and stitch "Visor" design onto baby visor, using two strands floss for Cross-Stitch and one strand floss for Backstitch.
3: For Shirt, center and stitch "Shirt" design onto baby T-shirt insert, using two strands floss for Cross-Stitch and one strand floss for Backstitch.
4: For Bottle Cover, center and stitch one Duck motif from "Shirt" graph onto baby bottle cover, using two strands floss for Cross-Stitch and one strand floss for Backstitch.

*101 Quick & Easy Cross-Stitch Projects*

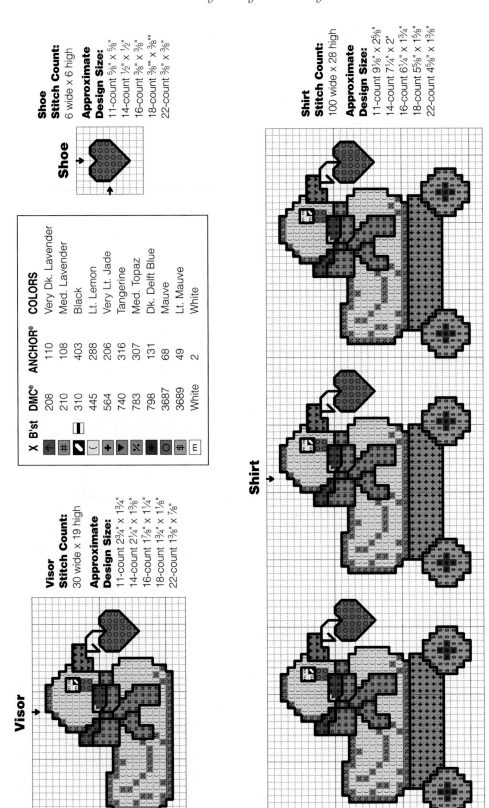

**Shoe**

**Stitch Count:** 6 wide x 6 high

**Approximate Design Size:**
11-count 5⁄8" x 5⁄8"
14-count 1⁄2" x 1⁄2"
16-count 3⁄8" x 3⁄8"
18-count 3⁄8" x 3⁄8"
22-count 3⁄8" x 3⁄8"

**Visor**

**Stitch Count:** 30 wide x 19 high

**Approximate Design Size:**
11-count 2¾" x 1¾"
14-count 2¼" x 1³⁄8"
16-count 1⁷⁄8" x 1¼"
18-count 1¾" x 1⁄8"
22-count 1³⁄8" x 7⁄8"

**Shirt**

**Stitch Count:** 100 wide x 28 high

**Approximate Design Size:**
11-count 9⅛" x 2⁵⁄8"
14-count 7¼" x 2"
16-count 6¼" x 1¾"
18-count 5⁵⁄8" x 1⁵⁄8"
22-count 4⁵⁄8" x 1³⁄8"

| X | B'st | DMC® | ANCHOR® | COLORS |
|---|---|---|---|---|
| | | 208 | 110 | Very Dk. Lavender |
| | | 210 | 108 | Med. Lavender |
| | | 310 | 403 | Black |
| | | 445 | 288 | Lt. Lemon |
| | | 564 | 206 | Very Lt. Jade |
| | | 740 | 316 | Tangerine |
| | | 783 | 307 | Med. Topaz |
| | | 798 | 131 | Dk. Delft Blue |
| | | 3687 | 68 | Mauve |
| | | 3689 | 49 | Lt. Mauve |
| | | White | 2 | White |

# Grandma Says

### DESIGNED BY CARLA ACOSTA

**G**randmas are very special people. Show your grandma how much you love her when you add this design to a photo album filled with wonderful memories.

## Materials

- 14" x 17" piece of white 14-count Aida
- Photo album
- Mounting board
- 1¼ yds. of piping
- Mounting board
- Craft glue or glue gun

## Instructions

1: Center and stitch design, using two strands floss for Cross-Stitch and one strand floss for Backstitch and French Knot of wording. Use one strand of floss for remaining Backstitch

Note: From mounting board, cut one 11¾" x 10½" piece.

2: Center and mount design over mounting board. Glue piping around outside edges of design. Position and glue mounted design to front of photo album as shown in photo.

**Stitch Count:**
146 wide x 116 high

**Approximate Design Size:**
11-count 10⅞" x 8¾"
14-count 8½" x 6⅞"
16-count 7½" x 6½"
18-count 6⅝" x 5⅜"
22-count 5½" x 4⅜"

| X | B'st | Fr | DMC® | ANCHOR® | COLORS |
|---|------|----|------|---------|--------|
| ✦✦ | | | 209 | 109 | Dk. Lavender |
| ◌ | | | 350 | 11 | Med. Coral |
| % | | | 704 | 256 | Bright Chartreuse |
| ) | | | 727 | 293 | Very Lt. Topaz |
| ✳ | | | 742 | 303 | Lt. Tangerine |
| # | | | 798 | 131 | Dk. Delft Blue |
| < | | | 813 | 161 | Lt. Blue |
| | ▬ | ● | 3371 | 382 | Black Brown |

# An Apple a Day

## Designed by Susan Stadler

Y*ou're sure to make an "A" when you give a special teacher this bookmark stitched in beautiful hand-dyed floss.*

## Materials

• Prefinished bookmark with lace with 1¾" x 6¾" white 18-count Aida design area

## Instructions

Center and stitch design, using two strands floss for Cross-Stitch.

| X | WEEKS DYE WORKS | DMC® | COLORS |
|---|---|---|---|
| ✚ | | 801 | Dk. Coffee Brown |
| ✳ | | 3346 | Hunter Green |
| # | 1113 | | Moonsglow |
| $ | 1336 | | Raspberry |
| ✘ | 2191 | | Granny Smith |

**Stitch Count:**
24 wide x 101 high

**Approximate Design Size:**
11-count 2¼" x 9¼"
14-count 1¾" x 7¼"
16-count 1½" x 6⅜"
18-count 1⅜" x 5⅝"
22-count 1⅛" x 4⅝"

# *Inch by Inch*

## DESIGNED BY MARY T. COSGROVE

**Y**our favorite little girl or boy will be the envy of the class with this fun learning accessory.

## *Materials*

- 2¼" x 12" acrylic ruler with white 14-count Vinyl-Weave™ insert

## *Instructions*

1: Center and stitch design onto insert, using two strands floss for Cross-Stitch, Backstitch and French Knot.

2: Assemble ruler following manufacturer's instructions.

**Stitch Count:**
149 wide x 17 high

**Approximate Design Size:**
11-count 13⅝" x 1⅝"
14-count 10¾" x 1¼"
16-count 9⅜" x 1½"
18-count 8⅜" x 1"
22-count 6⅞" x ⅞"

| X | B'st | Fr | DMC® | ANCHOR® | COLORS |
|---|---|---|---|---|---|
| | | ● | 310 | 403 | Black |
| + | | | 3832 | 38 | Med. Raspberry |
| ⦿ | | | 3843 | 410 | Electric Blue |

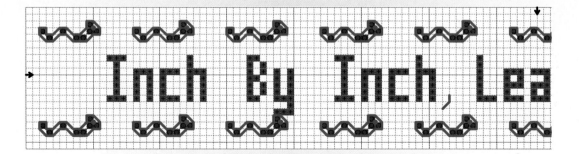

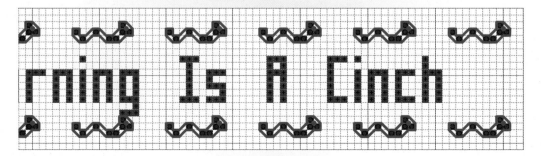

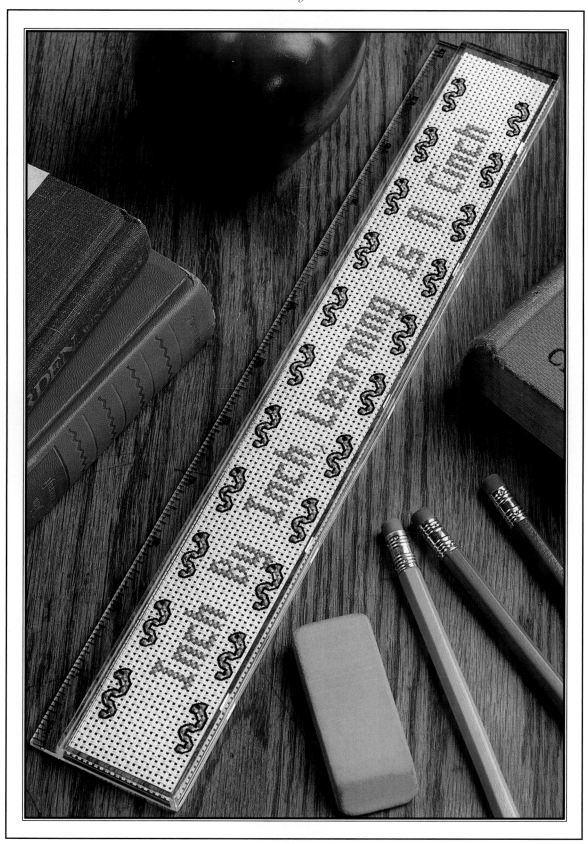

*101 Quick & Easy Cross-Stitch Projects*

# Wedding Sampler

## DESIGNED BY JULIA LUCAS

*Commemorate a special wedding day with this splendid announcement. Embellished with a floral garland, this elegant gift features the names of the bride and groom along with the date of their marriage. The wedding couple will treasure this guest book forever.*

## Materials

- 9" x 9" piece of white 28-count Jobelan®
- Mounting board
- Guest book
- Decorative trim
- Craft glue or glue gun

## Instructions

1: Select desired letters and numbers from Alphabet and Numbers graph for names and date, center and stitch design, stitching over two threads and using two strands floss for Cross-Stitch and one strand floss for Backstitch and French Knot.

Note: Trim design to desired size.

2: Center and mount design over mounting board. Glue decorative trim to outside edges of mounted design. Position and secure mounted design to front of guest book as shown in photo.

## Alphabet and Numbers

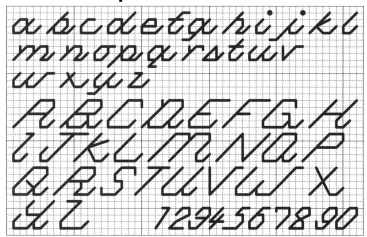

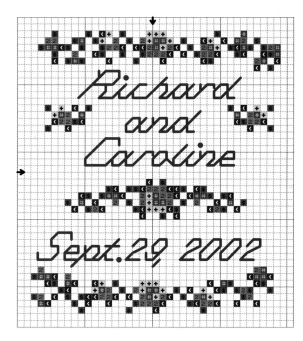

**Stitch Count:**
37 wide x 42 high

**Approximate Design Size:**
11-count 3⅜" x 3⅞"
14-count 2¾" x 3"
16-count 2⅜" x 2⅝"
18-count 2⅛" x 2⅜"
22-count 1¾" x 2"
22-count 1¾" x 2"
28-count over two threads 2¾" x 3"

| X | B'st | Fr | DMC® | ANCHOR® | COLORS |
|---|------|-----|------|---------|--------|
| ⊟ | ▬ | ● | 310 | 403 | Black |
| # | | | 326 | 59 | Very Dk. Rose |
| 2 | | | 961 | 76 | Dk. Dusty Rose |
| + | | | 963 | 73 | Ultra Very Lt. Dusty Rose |
| ‹ | | | 3362 | 263 | Dk. Pine Green |
| $ | | | 3363 | 262 | Med. Pine Green |

# Piano Lessons

## DESIGNED BY CAROL KROB

*C*arry everything *C*needed for a *successful music lesson in this harmonious tote bag.*

## Materials

- 15" x 11" natural canvas briefcase with handles
- 7" x 11" piece and six 4" x 4" pieces of 8.5-count waste canvas

## Instructions

1: Position and baste 7" x 11" piece and each 4" x 4" piece of waste canvas to front of briefcase according to Stitching Diagram. Center and stitch "Treble Clef" design onto 7" x 11" piece of waste canvas and

"Note" design onto each 4" x 4" piece of waste canvas; suing six strands floss for Cross-Stitch and two strands floss for Backstitch.

2: Remove waste canvas after stitching following manufacturer's instructions.

**Note**

**Stitching Diagram**

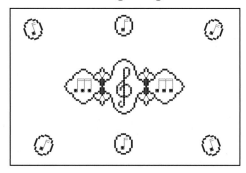

| X | B'st | DMC® | ANCHOR® | COLORS |
|---|------|------|---------|--------|
| ✚ | ▭ | 310 | 403 | Black |
| ◢ | ▭ | 312 | 979 | Very Dk. Baby Blue |
| # | | 349 | 13 | Dk. Coral |

**Note
Stitch Count:**
11 wide x 13 high

**Approximate
Design Size:**
8.5-count 1⅜" x 1⅝"
11-count 1" x 1¼"
14-count ⅞" x 1"
16-count ¾" x ⅞"
18-count ⅝" x ¾"
22-count ½" x ⅝"

**Treble Clef
Stitch Count:**
71 wide x 33 high

**Approximate
Design Size:**
8.5-count 8⅜" x 4"
11-count 6½" x 3"
14-count 5⅛" x 2⅜"
16-count 4½" x 2⅛"
18-count 4" x 1⅞"
22-count 3¼" x 1½"

**Treble Clef**

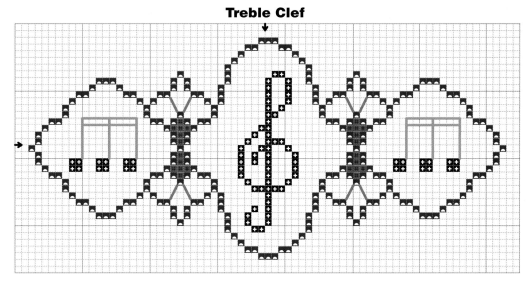

# *Antique Auto*

## DESIGNED BY LOIS WINSTON

A whimsical antique auto stitched on this address book insert makes the perfect traveling companion. You may need to make several — when your friends see it they'll all want one, too!

## *Materials*

- Address book with 4" x 6" white 14-count Vinyl-Weave™ insert

## *Instructions*

Center and stitch design, using two strands floss for Cross-Stitch and one strand floss for Backstitch. Assemble address book following manufacturer's instructions.

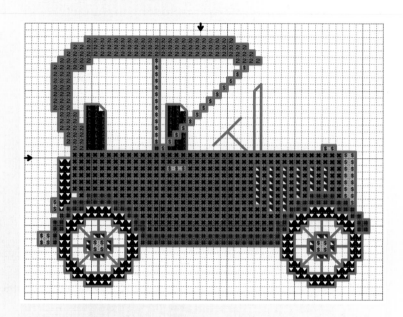

| X | B'st | DMC® | ANCHOR® | COLORS |
|---|---|---|---|---|
| ▼ | ▭ | 310 | 403 | Black |
| 0 | | 924 | 851 | Very Dk. Gray Green |
| # | | 926 | 850 | Med. Gray Green |
| $ | | 928 | 274 | Very Lt. Gray Green |
| 2 | | 3828 | 888 | Hazelnut Brown |
| ◣ | | 3847 | 189 | Dk. Teal Green |
| ✖ | | 3849 | 185 | Lt. Teal Green |

**Stitch Count:**
49 wide x 47 high

**Approximate Design Size:**
11-count 4½" x 3⅜"
14-count 3½" x 2¾"
16-count 3⅛" x 2⅜"
18-count 2¾" x 2⅛"
22-count 2¼" x 1¾"

# Romantic Wedding

## DESIGNED BY KATHLEEN HURLEY

*Stitch this romantic design with silver or gold floss to commemorate a 25th or 50th wedding anniversary. For the newlyweds, it's perfect stitched in colors to match the wedding celebration.*

## Materials

• 11" x 12" piece of white 28-count Jobelan®

**Stitch Count:**
81 wide x 72 high

**Approximate Design Size:**
11-count 7⅜" x 6⅝"
14-count 5⅞" x 5¼"
16-count 5⅛" x 4½"
18-count 4½" x 4"
22-count 3¾" x 3⅜"
28-count over two
 threads 5⅞" x 5¼"

## Instructions

Center and stitch design, stitching over two threads and using one strand floss for Cross-Stitch.

| X | TRUECOLORSTM (#14 PREBLENDED) | DMC® COLORS | |
|---|---|---|---|
| ◎ | TH30003 | 5284 | Gold |

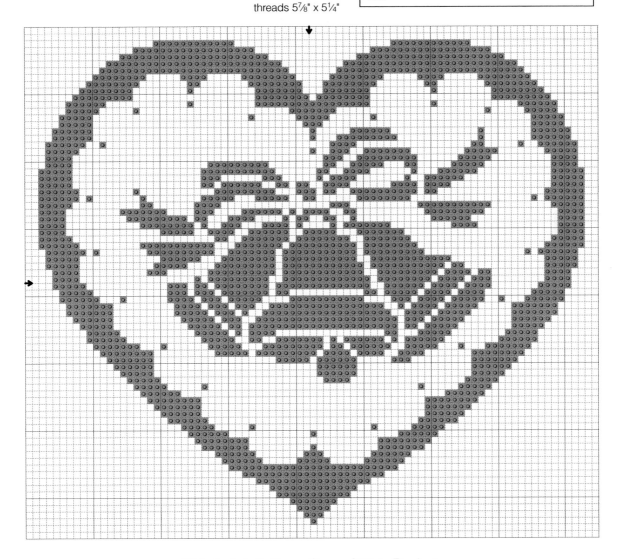

# Babykins

## DESIGNED BY HOPE MURPHY

What better reason to stitch than for a new baby? This diaper bag, towel and bib are cute and useful gifts that will be treasured always.

## Materials

- 15" x 25" Huck Showcase Towel with 4½" x 6" white 14-count Aida insert
- Fingertip towel with 2½" x 11" white 14-count Aida insert
- Baby bib with 2¼" x 10" white 14-count Aida insert
- ¼ yd. of lining fabric
- Interfacing
- 1 yd. of 1¼" webbing
- Two diaper pins

## Instructions

1: For Bag, center and stitch "Bag" design onto huck towel insert following Stitching Diagram, using three strands floss for Cross-Stitch and Backstitch of block pattern lines. Use one strand floss for remaining Backstitch and French Knot.

Notes: From lining fabric and interfacing, cut one each 15" x 25". Use ½" seam allowance.

2: For lining, apply interfacing to wrong side of lining fabric following manufacturer's instructions.

3: For handles, cut webbing in half. Position one handle to wrong side of each short edge on towel; secure in place.

4: With right sides facing, sew towel and lining together, leaving an opening for turning. Turn right sides out; slip stitch opening closed.

5: With right sides facing and matching short edges, sew towel together at sides, forming tote. Turn right sides out.

6: Attach diaper pins to front of tote as shown in photo.

7: For Fingertip Towel, center and stitch "Towel" design onto insert, using three strands floss for Cross-Stitch and Backstitch of block pattern lines. Use one strand floss for remaining Backstitch and French Knot.

8: For Bib, center and stitch "Bib" design onto insert, using three strands floss for Cross-Stitch and Backstitch of block pattern lines. Use one strand floss for remaining Backstitch and French Knot.

### Stitching Diagram

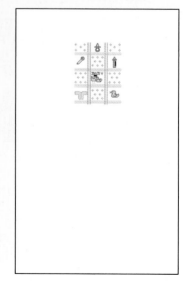

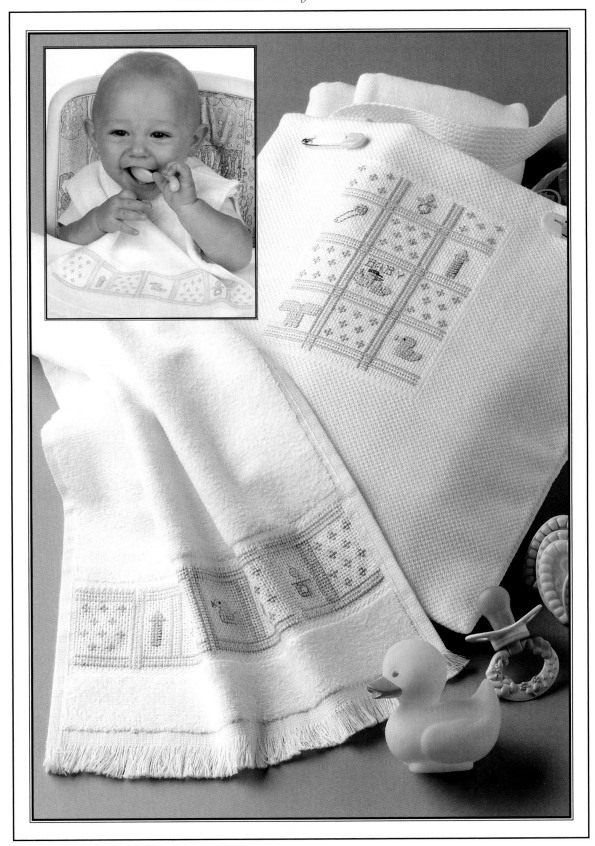

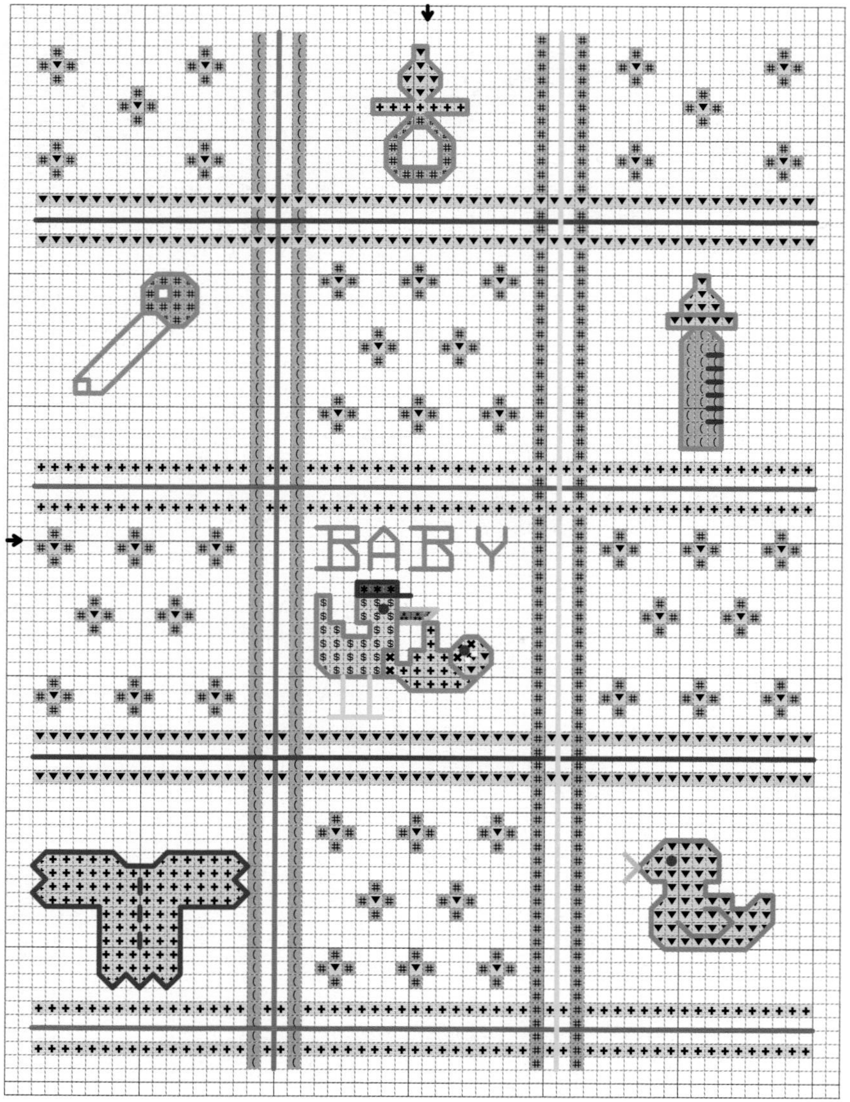

**Bag**
**Stitch Count:**
58 wide x 77 high

**Approximate Design Size:**
11-count 5⅜" x 7"
14-count 4¼" x 5½"
16-count 3⅝" x 4⅞"
18-count 3¼" x 3½"
22-count 2⅝" x 3½"

| X | B'st | Fr | DMC® | ANCHOR® | COLORS |
|---|------|----|----|------|--------|
| ● | | | 310 | 403 | Black |
| | | | 318 | 399 | Lt. Steel Gray |
| | | | 744 | 301 | Pale Yellow |
| | | | 818 | 23 | Baby Pink |
| | | | 819 | 271 | Lt. Baby Pink |
| | | | 955 | 206 | Lt. Nile Green |
| | | | 970 | 316 | Lt. Pumpkin |
| | | | 3761 | 928 | Lt. Sky Blue |
| | | | Ecru | 387 | Ecru |

**Bib**
**Stitch Count:**
134 wide x 29 high

**Approximate Design Size:**
11-count 12¼" x 2⅝"
14-count 9⅝" x 2⅛"
16-count 8⅜" x 1⅞"
18-count 7½" x 1⅝"
22-count 6⅛" x 1⅜"

**Towel**
**Stitch Count:**
137 wide x 29 high

**Approximate Design Size:**
11-count 12½" x 2⅝"
14-count 9⅞" x 2⅛"
16-count 8⅝" x 1⅞"
18-count 7⅝" x 1⅝"
22-count 6¼" x 1⅜"

**Bag**

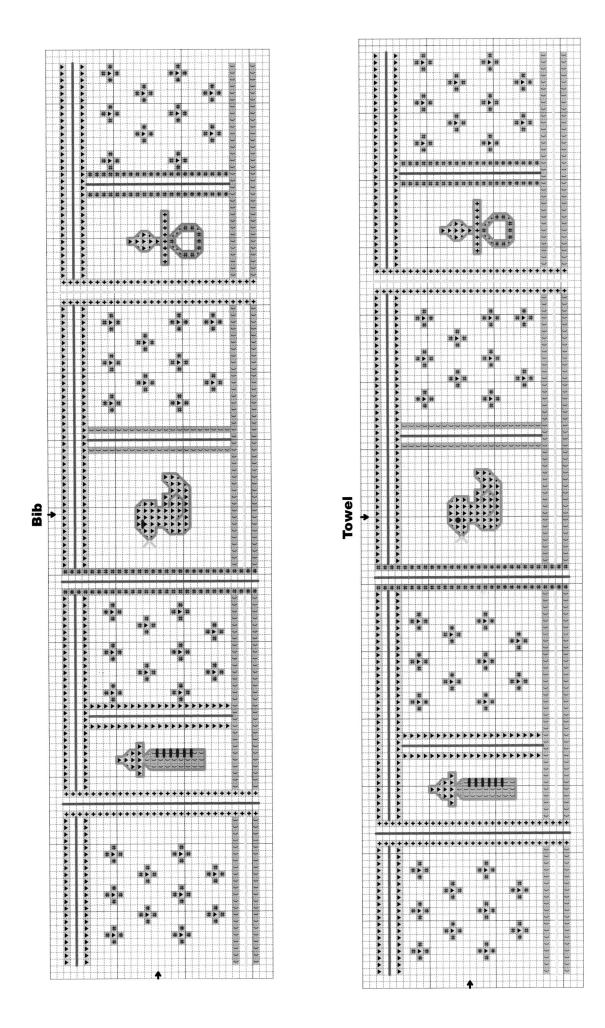

**Bib**

**Towel**

# Pansy Border

## DESIGNED BY LISA MESSEGEE

*Stylized pansies make a unique border trim. Personalize this framed piece by adding a favorite photograph to the center area. Make a coordinating candle wrap as a quick gift or to add to the frame.*

## Materials

• One 11" x 11" piece and one 7" x 14" piece of white 14-count Aida

## Instructions

1: For Frame, center and stitch "Frame" design onto 11" x 11" piece of Aida, using two strands floss for Cross-Stitch.

Note: Photo could be secured to center of design if desired.

2: For Candle Wrap, center and stitch "Candle" design onto 7" x 14" piece of Aida, using two strands floss for Cross-Stitch. Trim stitched design to 1¾" x desired length. Stay stitch one square from stitched design on long edges; fray edges.

**Frame**

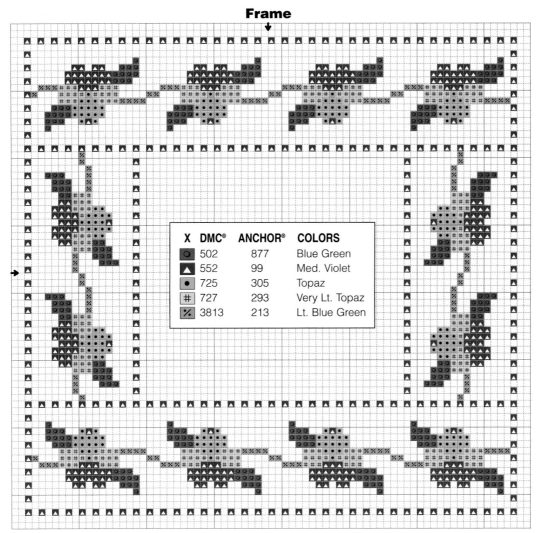

**Frame Stitch Count:**
73 wide x 71 high

**Approximate Design Size:**
11-count 6⅝" x 6½"
14-count 5¼" x 5⅛"
16-count 4⅝" x 4½"
18-count 4⅛" x 4"
22-count 3⅜" x 3¼"

| X | DMC® | ANCHOR® | COLORS |
|---|------|---------|--------|
| ○ | 502 | 877 | Blue Green |
| ▲ | 552 | 99 | Med. Violet |
| • | 725 | 305 | Topaz |
| # | 727 | 293 | Very Lt. Topaz |
| ⁒ | 3813 | 213 | Lt. Blue Green |

**Candle Stitch Count:**
108 wide x 17 high

**Approximate Design Size:**
11-count 9⅞" x 1⅝"
14-count 7¾" x 1¼"
16-count 6¾" x 1⅛"
18-count 6" x 1"
22-count 5" x ⅞"

**Candle**

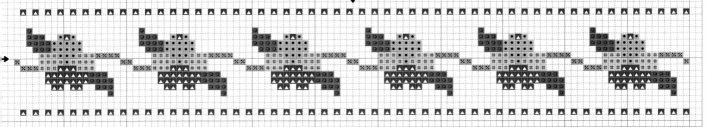

# A Mother's Love

## DESIGNED BY MIKE VICKERY

*Sometimes a picture is worth a thousand words. This simple and pretty piece is one that a mother will treasure.*

## Materials

• 12" x 13" piece of buttermilk 28-count Jobelan®

## Instructions

Center and stitch design, stitching over two threads and using two strands floss for Cross-Stitch and one strand floss for Backstitch.

| X | B'st | DMC® | ANCHOR® | COLORS |
|---|------|------|---------|--------|
| | ▭ | 319 | 218 | Very Dk. Pistachio Green |
| | ▭ | 333 | 119 | Very Dk. Blue Violet |
| ▣ | | 335 | 38 | Rose |
| + | | 341 | 117 | Lt. Blue Violet |
| ▬ | | 368 | 214 | Lt. Pistachio Green |
| ^ | | 369 | 1043 | Very Lt. Pistachio Green |
| Y | | 727 | 293 | Very Lt. Topaz |
| n | | 776 | 24 | Med. Pink |
| ) | | 818 | 23 | Baby Pink |
| # | | 899 | 52 | Med. Rose |
| | ▭ | 961 | 76 | Dk. Dusty Rose |
| o | | 3747 | 120 | Very Lt. Blue Violet |
| · | | White | 2 | White |

**Stitch Count:**
100 wide x 80 high

**Approximate Design Size:**
11-count 9⅛" x 7⅜"
14-count 7¼" x 5¾"
16-count 6¼" x 5"
18-count 5⅝" x 4½"
22-count 4⅝" x 3⅝"
28-count over two
 threads 7¼" x 5¾"

# Holiday Angels

## DESIGNED BY ORIGINAL BY ANNIE

An angel with a quick-to-stitch Valentine, Saint Patrick's Day or Fourth of July motif makes the perfect holiday accent. These sweet linen angels can also be displayed year-round.

## Materials for One

• Brianna pull apart kit with 28-count Linen look tea towel

## Instructions

Note: Assemble Kit following manufacturer's instructions.

Center and stitch design of choice, stitching over two threads and using two strands floss for Cross-Stitch.

**Flag**

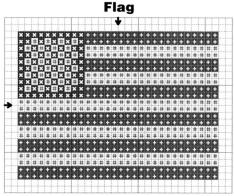

| X | DMC® | ANCHOR® | COLORS |
|---|------|---------|--------|
| ✗ | 312 | 979 | Very Dk. Baby Blue |
| ✚ | 321 | 9046 | Red |
| $ | 601 | 57 | Dk. Cranberry |
| ℀ | 701 | 227 | Lt. Green |
| # | White | 2 | White |

**Flag**
**Stitch Count:**
30 wide x 22 high

**Approximate Design Size:**
11-count 2¾" x 2"
14-count 2¼" x 1⅝"
16-count 1⅞" x 1⅜"
18-count 1¾" x 1¼"
22-count 1⅜" x 1"
28-count over two
  threads 2¼" x 1⅝"

| X | DMC® | ANCHOR® | COLORS |
|---|---|---|---|
| ✖ | 312 | 979 | Very Dk. Baby Blue |
| ✚ | 321 | 9046 | Red |
| ▦ | 601 | 57 | Dk. Cranberry |
| ◪ | 701 | 227 | Lt. Green |
| # | White | 2 | White |

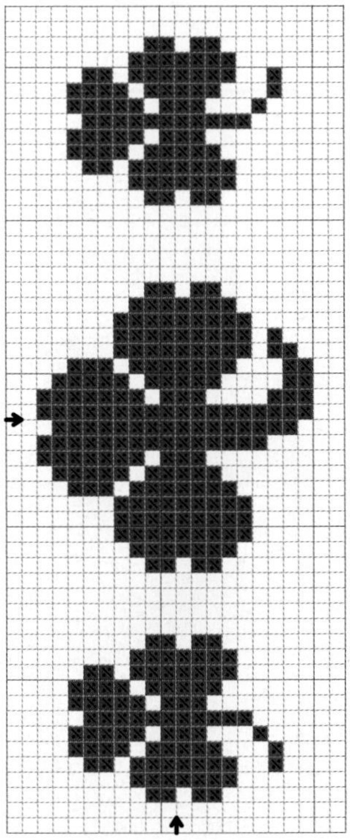

**Hearts**
**Stitch Count:**
34 wide x 11 high

**Approximate
Design Size:**
11-count 3⅛" x 1"
14-count 2½" x ⅞"
16-count 2⅛" x ¾"
18-count 2" x ⅝"
22-count 1⅝" x ½"
28-count over two
threads 2½" x ⅞"

**Hearts**

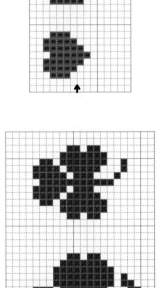

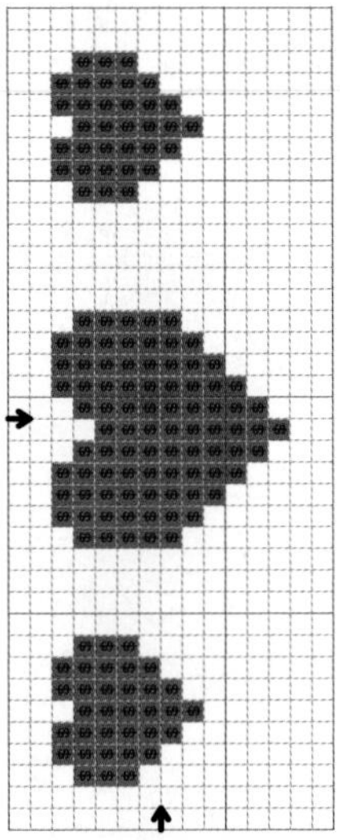

**Shamrocks
Stitch Count:**
50 wide x 18 high

**Approximate
Design Size:**
11-count 4⅝" x 1⅝"
14-count 3⅝" x 1⅜"
16-count 3⅛" x 1⅛"
18-count 2⅞" x 1"
22-count 2⅜" x ⅞"
28-count over two
threads 3⅝" x 1⅜"

**Shamrocks**

*General*

*Instructions*

## *Tools of the Stitcher*

### Fabrics

Most counted cross-stitch projects are worked on even-weave fabrics made especially for counted thread embroidery. These fabrics have vertical and horizontal threads of uniform thickness and spacing. Aida cloth is a favorite of beginning stitchers because its weave forms distinctive squares in the fabric, which makes placing stitches easy. To determine a fabric's thread count, count the number of threads per inch of fabric.

Linen is made from fibers of the flax plant and is strong and durable. Its lasting quality makes it the perfect choice for heirloom projects. Linen is available in a range of muted colors and stitch counts.

In addition to evenweave fabrics, many stitchers enjoy using waste canvas and perforated paper. Waste canvas is basted to clothing or other fabric, forming a grid for stitching which is later removed. Perforated paper has holes evenly spaced for 14 stitches per inch.

### Needles

Cross-stitch needles should have elongated eyes and blunt points. They should slip easily between the threads of the fabric, but should not pierce the fabric. The most common sizes used for cross-stitching are size 24 or 26. The ideal needle size is just small enough to slip easily through your fabric. Some stitchers prefer to use a slightly smaller needle for backstitching. When stitching on waste canvas, use a sharp needle.

### Hoops, Frames & Scissors

Hoops can be round or oval and come in many sizes. The three main types are plastic, spring-tension and wooden. Frames are easier on the fabric than hoops and come in many sizes and shapes. Once fabric is mounted it doesn't have to be removed until stitching is complete, saving fabric from excessive handling.

Small, sharp scissors are essential for cutting floss and removing mistakes. For cutting fabrics, invest in a top-quality pair of medium-sized sewing scissors. To keep them in top form, use these scissors only for cutting fabrics and floss.

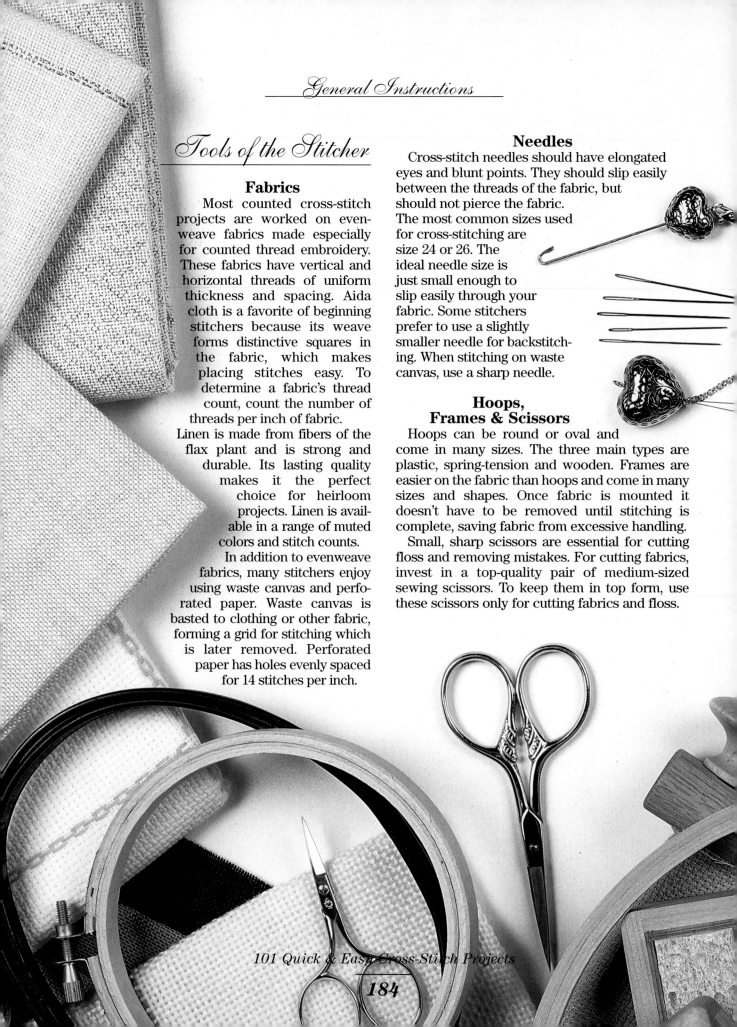

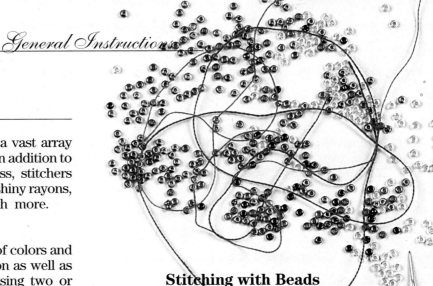

# Stitching Threads

Today's cross-stitcher can achieve a vast array of effects in texture, color and shine. In addition to the perennial favorite, six-strand floss, stitchers can choose from sparkling metallics, shiny rayons, silks, narrow ribbon threads and much more.

### Six-Strand Floss

Six-strand floss comes in a variety of colors and is available in metallics, silk and rayon as well as cotton. Most projects are worked using two or three strands of floss for cross-stitches and one or two strands for backstitches. For ease of stitching and to prevent wear on fibers, use lengths no longer than 18".

### Pearl Cotton

Pearl cotton is available in #3, #5, #8 and #12, with #3 being the thickest. The plies of pearl cotton will not separate, and for most stitching one strand is used. Pearl cotton has a lustrous sheen.

### Flower & Ribbon Threads

Flower thread has a tight twist and comes in many soft colors. It is heavier than one ply of six-strand floss – one strand of flower thread equals two strands of floss. Ribbon thread is a narrow ribbon especially created for stitching. It comes in a large number of colors in satin as well as metallic finishes.

### Blending Filament & Metallic Braid

Blending filament is a fine, shiny fiber that can be used alone or combined with floss or other thread. Knotting the blending filament on the needle with a slipknot is recommended for control.

Metallic braid is a braided metallic fiber, usually used single-ply. Thread this fiber just as you would any other fiber. Use short lengths, about 15", to keep the fiber from fraying.

**SLIPKNOT**

### Stitching with Beads

Small seed beads can be added to any cross-stitch design, using one bead per stitch. Knot thread at beginning of beaded section for security, especially if you are adding beads to clothing. The bead should lie in the same direction as the top half of cross-stitches.

### Bead Attachment

Use one strand floss to secure beads. Bring beading needle up from back of work, leaving 2" length of thread hanging; do not knot (end will be secured between stitches as you work). Thread bead on needle; complete stitch.

Do not skip over more than two stitches or spaces without first securing thread, or last bead will be loose. To secure, weave thread into several stitches on back of work. Follow graph to work design, using one bead per stitch.

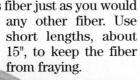

# Before You Begin

Assemble fabric, floss, pattern and tools. Familiarize yourself with the graph, color key and instructions before beginning.

## Preparing Fabric

Before you stitch, decide how large to cut fabric. If you are making a pillow or other design which requires a large unstitched area, be sure to leave plenty of fabric. If you are making a small project, leave at least 3" around all edges of design. Determine the design area size by using this formula: number of stitches across design area divided by the number of threads per inch of fabric equals size of fabric in inches. Measure fabric, then cut evenly along horizontal and vertical threads.

Press out folds. To prevent raveling, hand overcast or machine zigzag fabric edges. Find center of fabric by folding horizontally and vertically and mark with a small stitch.

## Reading Graphs

Cross-stitch graphs or charts are made up of colors and symbols to tell you the exact color, type and placement of each stitch. Each square represents the area for one complete cross-stitch. Next to each graph, there is a key with information about stitches and floss colors represented by the graph's colors and symbols.

Color keys have abbreviated headings for cross-stitch (x), one-half cross-stitch (½x), quarter cross-stitch (¼x), three-quarter cross-stitch (¾x), back-stitch (B'st), French knot (Fr), lazy daisy stitch (LzD) and straight stitch (Str). Some graphs are so large they must be divided for printing.

## Preparing Floss

The six strands of floss are easily separated, and the number of strands used is given in instructions. Cut strands in 14"-18" lengths. When separating floss, always separate all six strands, then recombine the number of strands needed. To make floss separating easier, run cut length across a damp sponge. To prevent floss from tangling, run cut length through a fabric-softener dryer sheet before separating and threading needle. To colorfast red floss tones, which sometimes bleed, hold floss under running water until water runs clear. Allow to air dry.

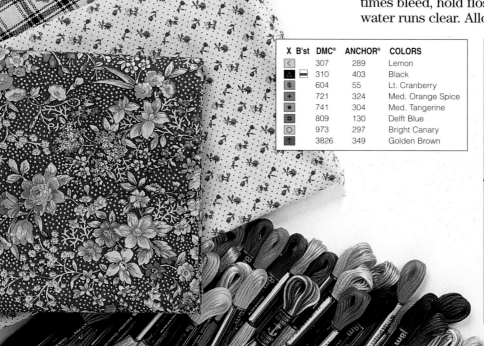

| X | B'st | DMC® | ANCHOR® | COLORS |
|---|---|---|---|---|
| < | | 307 | 289 | Lemon |
| △ | ▭ | 310 | 403 | Black |
| $ | | 604 | 55 | Lt. Cranberry |
| + | | 721 | 324 | Med. Orange Spice |
| ★ | | 741 | 304 | Med. Tangerine |
| # | | 809 | 130 | Delft Blue |
| ○ | | 973 | 297 | Bright Canary |
| ↑ | | 3826 | 349 | Golden Brown |

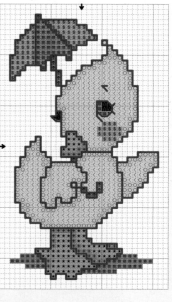

# *Stitching Techniques*

### Beginning & Ending a Thread

Try these methods for beginning a thread, then decide which one is best for you.

1: *Securing the thread*: Start by pulling needle through fabric back to front, leaving about 1" behind fabric. Hold this end with fingers as you begin stitching, and work over end with your first few stitches. After work is in progress, weave end through the back of a few stitches.

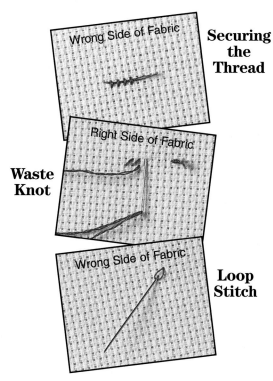

**Securing the Thread**

Wrong Side of Fabric

**Waste Knot**

Right Side of Fabric

**Loop Stitch**

Wrong Side of Fabric

2: *Waste knot*: Make a knot in end of floss and pull needle through fabric front to back several squares over from where your first cross-stitch will be. Come up at first stitch and stitch first few stitches over floss end. Clip knot.

3: *Loop stitch*: This method can only be used for even numbers of strands. Cut strands twice the normal length, then take half the number of strands needed and fold in half. Insert loose ends in needle and bring needle up from back at first stitch, leaving loop underneath. Take needle down through fabric and through loop; pull to secure.

For even stitches, keep a consistent tension on your thread, and pull thread and needle completely through fabric with each stab of the needle.

Make all the top crosses on your cross-stitches face the same direction. To finish a thread, run the needle under the back side of several stitches and clip. Threads carried across the back of unworked areas may show through to the front, so do not carry threads.

### Master Stitchery

Work will be neater if you always try to make each stitch by coming up in an unoccupied hole and going down in an occupied hole.

The sewing method is preferred for stitching on linen and some other evenweaves, but can also be used on Aida. Stitches are made as in hand sewing with needle going from front to back to front of fabric in one motion. All work is done from the front of the fabric. When stitching with the sewing method, it is important not to pull thread too tightly or stitches will become distorted. Stitching on linen is prettiest with the sewing method, using no hoop. If you use a hoop or frame when using the sewing method with Aida, keep in mind that fabric cannot be pulled taut. There must be "give" in the fabric in order for needle to slip in and out easily.

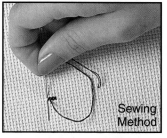

Sewing Method

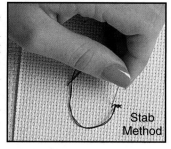

Stab Method

In the stab method, needle and floss are taken completely through fabric twice with each stitch. For the first half of the stitch, bring needle up and pull thread completely through fabric to the front. Then take needle down and reach underneath and pull completely through to bottom.

### Working on Evenweave

When working on linen or other evenweave fabric, keep needle on right side of fabric, taking needle front to back to front with each stitch. Work

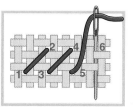

over two threads, placing the beginning and end of the bottom half of the first Cross-Stitch where a vertical thread crosses a horizontal thread.

# *Framing and Mounting*

## Shopping for Frames

When you shop for a frame, take the stitchery along with you and compare several frame and mat styles. Keep in mind the "feeling" of your stitched piece when choosing a frame. For example, an exquisite damask piece stitched with metallics and silk threads might need an ornate gold frame, while a primitive sampler stitched on dirty linen with flower thread would need a simpler, perhaps wooden frame.

## Mounting

Cross-stitch pieces can be mounted on mat board, white cardboard, special padded or unpadded mounting boards designed specifically for needlework, or special acid-free mat board available from art supply stores. Acid-free framing materials are the best choice for projects you wish to keep well-preserved for future generations. If you prefer a padded look, cut quilt batting to fit mounting board.

Center blocked stitchery over mounting board of choice with quilt batting between, if desired. Leaving 1½" to 3" around all edges, trim excess fabric away along straight grain.

Mounting boards made for needlework have self-stick surfaces and require no pins. When using these products, lift and smooth needlework onto board until work is taut and edges are smooth and even. Turn board face down and smooth fabric to back, mitering corners.

Pins are required for other mounting boards. With design face up, keeping fabric straight and taut, insert a pin through fabric and edge of mounting board at the center of each side. Turn piece face down and smooth excess fabric to back, mitering corners.

There are several methods for securing fabric edges. Edges may be glued to mat board with liquid fabric glue or fabric glue stick. If mat board is thick, fabric may be stapled.

## Mats & Glass

Pre-cut mats are available in many sizes and colors to fit standard-size frames. Custom mats are available in an even wider variety of colors, textures and materials. Using glass over cross-stitch is a matter of personal preference, but is generally discouraged. Moisture can collect behind glass and rest on fabric, causing mildew stains. A single or double mat will hold glass away from fabric.

# *Cleaning Your Needlework*

Careful washing, pressing and sometimes blocking help preserve and protect your stitched piece. After stitching is complete, a gentle washing will remove surface dirt, hoop marks and hand oils that have accumulated on your fabric while stitching. Even if a piece looks clean, it's always a good idea to give it a nice cleaning before finishing. Never press your work before cleaning, as this only serves to set those hoop marks and soils that are best removed.

Using a gentle soap such as baby shampoo or gentle white dishwashing liquid and a large, clean bowl, make a solution of cool, sudsy water. If you use a handwash product, make sure the one you choose contains no chlorine bleach. Fill another bowl or sink with plain cool water for rinsing.

Soak your stitched piece in sudsy water for five to ten minutes. Then gently and without rubbing or twisting, squeeze suds through fabric several times. Dip piece several times in fresh cool water until no suds remain.

On rare occasions floss colors will run or fade slightly. When this happens, continue to rinse in cool water until water becomes perfectly clear. Remove fabric from water and lay on a soft, white towel. Never twist or wring your work. Blot excess water away and roll the piece up in the towel, pressing gently.

Never allow a freshly washed piece of embroidery to air dry. Instead, remove the damp piece from the towel and place face down on a fresh, dry white towel. To prevent color stains, it's important to keep the stitched piece flat, not allowing stitched areas to touch each other or other areas of the fabric. Make sure the edges of fabric are in straight lines and even. To be sure fabric edges are straight when pressing dry, use a ruler or T-square to check edges. Wash towel several times before using it to block cross-stitch, and use it only for this purpose.

After edges are aligned and fabric is perfectly smooth, cover the back of the stitched piece with a pressing cloth, cotton diaper or other lightweight white cotton cloth. Press dry with a dry iron set on a high permanent press or cotton setting, depending on fabric content. Allow stitchery to lie in this position several hours. Machine drying is acceptable after use for items like towels and kitchen accessories, but your work will be prettier and smoother if you give these items a careful pressing the first time.

# *Stitch Guide*

## **Basic Stitchery**

**Cross-Stitch (x):** There are two ways of making a basic Cross-Stitch. The first method is used when working rows of stitches in the same color. The first step makes the bottom half of the stitches across the row, and the second step makes the top half.

The second method is used when making single stitches. The bottom and top halves of each stitch are worked before starting the next stitch.

**Quarter Cross-Stitch (¼x):** Stitch may slant in any direction.

**Half Cross-Stitch (½x):** The first part of a Cross-Stitch. May slant in either direction.

**Three-Quarter Cross-Stitch (¾x):** A Half Cross-Stitch plus a Quarter Cross-Stitch. May slant in any direction.

# Embellishing with Embroidery

**EMBROIDERY** stitches add detail and dimension to stitching. Unless otherwise noted, work Backstitches first, then other embroidery stitches.

**Smyrna Cross Modified (SmyM)**

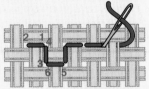

**Backstitch (B'st)**

**Spider Web Rose:** Stitch a 5-spoke web with (A). Run needle with floss up through center of web; keeping floss loose and allowing it to twist, weave floss over one spoke and under one spoke filling spokes completely (B), then run needle back to back of fabric at edge of rose.

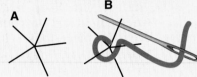

A                B

**French Knot (Fr)**

**Running Stitch (Run)**

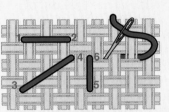

**Straight Stitch (Str)**

**Lazy Daisy Stitch (LzD)**

# Special Stitches

## Hemstitch

Step 1

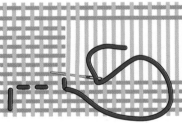

Wrong side of fabric.

Step 2

Wrong side of fabric.

Step 3

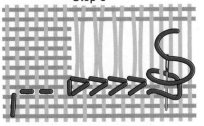

Wrong side of fabric.

Step 4

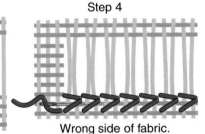

Wrong side of fabric.

Finished Hemstitch

Right side of fabric.

## Rhodes Stitch Variation (RhV)

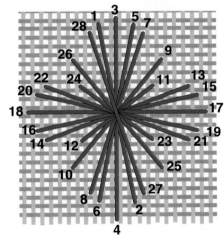

## Rhodes Heart (RhH)

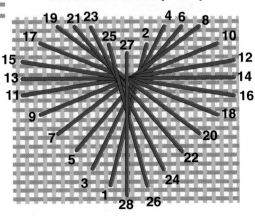

## Rhodes Heart Modified (Rhm)

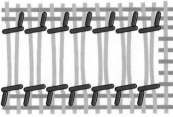

# Acknowledgments

**BagWorks;** 3301-C S. Cravens, Rd.; Ft Worth, TX 76119; Phone 800-365-7423:
**Apron:** Baking for Christmas
**Briefcase With Handles:** Piano Lessons
**Paperback Book Cover:** Symbols of Faith
**Zip Top Tote:** Sew Much Love

**Caron Collection;** 55 Old South Avenue; Stratford, CT 06615; Phone 800-862-2766:
**Watercolors®:** Hearts and Flowers

**Charles Craft, Inc.;** For further information call 800-277-0980:
**Aida:** God Bless America; Hummingbird Coasters; Pansy Border; A Colorful Easter
**"Baby Soft" Infant Bib:** Pretty Baby
**Bookmark:** An Apple a Day: Symbols of Faith
**Bread Cover:** Autumn Harvest
**Deluxe Baby Bib:** Babykins
**Fiddler's Cloth:** Wild Ducks
**Jar Lid Cover:** Treat Toppers
**Kitchenmate Towel:** Jardiniere Kitchen Set
**Showcase Huck Towel:** Babykins; Let It Snow; Handy Totes
**Velour Fingertip Towel:** Babykins; Watermelon Summer

**Creative Beginnings;** P.O. Box 1330; Morro Bay, CA 93443; Phone 800-367-1739:
**Charm:** Seasonal Needlerolls

**Daniel Enterprises;** 306 McKay Street; P.O. Box 1105; Laurinburg, NC 28353; Phone 910-277-7441:
**Address Book:** Antique Auto; Sampler Address Book
**Crafter's Pride Alma Lynne Christmas Tree Towel:** Oh Christmas Tree
**Crafter's Pride Baby Bottle Cover:** Everything's Duckie
**Crafter's Pride Mugs Your Way:** Merry Christmas
**Crafter's Pride Small Oval Addition:** Oh Christmas Tree
**Crafter's Pride Dispenser:** Bathroom Fishes
**Crafter's Pride Stitch-A-Caddy:** Wild Ducks
**Crafter's Pride Stitch-A-Ruler:** Inch by Inch
**Crafter's Pride Toothbrush Caddy:** Bathroom Fishes

**Delta Technical Coatings Inc.:** 2550 Pellissier Pl.; Whittier, CA 90601; Phone 800-423-4135:
**Stitchless® Glue:** Merry Christmas

**The DMC® Corporation;** 10 Port Kearny; South Kearny, NJ 07032-4688:

**Embroidery Floss:** A Colorful Easter; A Gardener's Delight; A Mother's Love; Antique Auto; Autumn Harvest; Autumn Mallards; Babykins; Baking for Christmas; Balloons; Baroque Noel; Bathroom Fishes; Blocks; Bountiful Cornucopia; Coffee Break; Dapper Duck; Delilah; Dutch Tulips; Eagle Spirit; Easter Flowers; Everything's Duckie; Feathered Family; Floral Essence; God Bless America; Grandma Says; Handy Totes; Holiday Angels; Holiday Pals; Hummingbird Coasters; Inch By Inch; Iris Studies; Land That I Love; Let It Snow; Lighthouses; Merry Christmas; Merry Christmas Tray; My Lady's Roses; Oh Christmas Tree; Pansy Border; Patriotic Checkers; Piano Lessons; Poinsettia Stocking; Roses and Violets; Safari Pillows; Sampler Address Book; Santa's On His Way; Sew Much Love; Sleep Tight; Snow Bunnies; Snowmen at Play; Snowman Minis; Spectator Sports; Star Snowmen; Stenciled Bouquet; Symbols of Faith; Treat Toppers; Watermelon Summer; Wedding Sampler; Welcome Irises; Wild Ducks; Witchy Moon
**Perle Coton (#3):** Celestial Dreams; Reindeer Draft Dodger

**Fairfield Processing Corp.;** Department W; P. O. Box 1157; Danbury, CT 06813; Phone 800-980-8000:
**Pop-In-Pillow Insert:** Safari Pillows
**Soft Touch Pillow Form:** Stenciled Bouquet

**Homespun Elegance Ltd.;** 11047 Pierson Dr., Ste 1; Fredericksburg, VA 22408; Phone 800-345-6471:
**Charm:** Seasonal Needlerolls

**Just Nan, Inc.;** 2300 Bethelview Road, Suite 110-402; Cumming, GA 30040; Phone 888-494-0361:
**Charm:** Seasonal Needlerolls

**KITI Inc.;** 300 N. Seminary Ave; Woodstock, IL 60098-0368; Phone 815-338-7970:
**Decorator Lamp Shade:** Blocks

**Kreinik Mfg. Co., Inc.;** 3106 Timanus Lane, Suite 101; Baltimore, MD 21244; Phone 800-537-2166:
**Silk Mori®:** Seasonal Needlerolls

**M.C.G. Textiles;** 13845 Magnolia Avenue, Chino, CA 91710; Phone 800-856-2499:
**Aida:** Reindeer Draft Dodger
**Blank Trivets:** Coffee Break
**Tear Away™ Canvas:** A Gardener's Delight; Autumn Mallards; Baking for Christmas; Dapper Duck; Dutch Tulips; Eagle Spirit; Fleurs-de-lys; Pretty Baby;

My Lady's Roses; Piano Lessons; Roses and Violets; Santa's On His Way; Snowman Minis; Star Snowmen; Symbols of Faith;
**White Tennis:** Everything's Duckie
**White T-Shirt:** Everything's Duckie
**Visor:** Everything's Duckie

**Gay Bowles Sales, Inc.;** P.O. Box 1060; Jamesville, WI 53547; Phone 800-356-9438:
**Mill Hill Seed Beads:** Star Snowmen
**Mill Hill Petite Beads:** Seasonal Needlerolls
**Mill Hill Stitchband:** Bathroom Fishes

**Freudenberg Pellon Nonwovens;** 3440 Industrial Dr.; Eno Industrial Park; Durham, NC 27704; Phone 919-620-3942:
**Fusible Fleece:** Safari Pillows

**Rushwear Apparel Mfg., Inc.;** P.O. Box 1352; Madison, WI 53701; Phone 800-739-6951:
**Stitch-A-Blouse:** My Lady's Roses

**Sudberry House;** 12 Colton Road; East Lyme, CT 06333; Phone 860-739-6951:
**Long Desk Box:** Patriotic Checkers
**Recipe Box:** Feathered Family
**Noteboard:** Feathered Family
**Round Pincushion:** Iris Studies
**Small Classic Tray:** Merry Christmas Tray; Patriotic Checkers
**Shaker Clock:** Welcome Irises
**Sharon Box:** Wild Ducks
**Square Oak Box:** Hearts and Flowers

**True Colors;** products available from Annie's Attic; Phone 800-LV-ANNIE:
**Pre-Blended Thread:** Romantic Wedding

**Weeks Dye Works;** 1510 Mechanical Blvd., Suite 103; Garner, NC 27529; Phone 919-722-9166:
**Over Dyed Floss:** An Apple A Day

**Westrim® Crafts/Western® Trimming Corp.;** 9667 Canoga Ave.; Chatsworth, CA 91311; Phone 818-998-8550:
**Fun Foam®:** Merry Christmas

**Wichelt Imports, Inc.;** products available from Needle Art Services; P.O. Box 2122; La Crosse, WI 54602-2122:
**Aida:** Blocks; Lighthouses
**Betsy Ross Linen:** Hearts and Flowers
**Jobelan:** Romantic Wedding; Mother's Love; Wedding Sampler
**Stitchband:** Seasonal Needlerolls

**Wimpole Street Creations;** 419 West 500 South; Bountiful, UT 84010; Phone 801-298-0504:

*continued on next page*

## Acknowledgments, cont'd

**Waffle Weave and Crochet Baby Afghan:** Sleep Tight
**Brianna Pull-Apart Kit:** Holiday Angels

**Wrights;** 85 South St.; West Warren, MA 01092; Phone 800-628-9362:
**Piping:** Safari Pillows

**X-Stitch Enterprises;** P. O. Box 5043-TCSJ01; Round Rock, TX 78683; Phone 512-251-2066:
**Stocking:** Poinsettia Stocking

**Yarn Tree Designs;** 117 Alexander Ave.; Ames, IA 50010; Phone 515-232-3121:
**Acrylic Coasters:** Hummingbird

Coasters
**Glass Paperweight:** Wild Ducks
**Needlework Card:** Balloons
**Pre-finished Pillow Sham:** Land That I Love
**Star Tree:** A Colorful Easter

**Zweigart®;** Products available from Needleworker's Delight; 121 Arthur Ave.; Colonia, NJ 07067; Phone 800-931-4545:
**Aida:** Bountiful Cornucopia; Feathered Family; Grandma Says; Merry Christmas Tray; Patriotic Checkers; Sew Much Love; Snowman Minis

**Country Aida:** Delilah
**Davosa®:** Snow Bunnies
**Diana:** Jardiniere Kitchen Set
**Edinburgh Linen:** Iris Studies
**Hearthside®:** Spectator Sports
**Klostern®:** Baroque Noel
**Lincoln:** Floral Essence; Safari Pillows
**Lugana:** Holiday Pals; Welcome Irises
**Meran:** Stenciled Bouquet
**Rustico Aida®:** Bountiful Cornucopia
**Stitchband:** Easter Flowers; Iris Studies; Watermelon Summer
**Tannenbaum:** Snowmen at Play
**Tula:** Celestial Dreams
**Vienna:** Coffee Break; Witchy Moon

# Pattern Index

# Designer Index